SECRETS OF SELF-MADE MILLIONAIRES

CRACK THE CODE TO GREATER WEALTH, HEALTH, AND HAPPINESS

MATTHEW R. KRATTER

WWW.TRADER.UNIVERSITY

CONTENTS

For my wife and children

DISCLAIMER

Neither Little Cash Machines LLC, nor any of its directors, officers, shareholders, personnel, representatives, agents, or independent contractors (collectively, the "Operator Parties") are licensed financial advisers, registered investment advisers, or registered broker-dealers. None of the Operator Parties are providing investment, financial, legal, or tax advice, and nothing in this book or at www.Trader.University (henceforth, "the Site") should be construed as such by you. This book and the Site should be used as educational tools only and are not replacements for professional investment advice.

This book also presents a wide range of opinions about a variety of topics related to health and well-being. These opinions reflect the research and ideas of the author or those whom the author has interviewed for this book, but these opinions are not intended to substitute for the services of a trained health care practitioner. Consult with your health care practitioner before engaging in any diet, drug, or exercise regime.

The author and the publisher disclaim responsibility for any adverse effects resulting directly or indirectly from information contained in this book.

The drugs discussed in this book may or may not be legal in your particular jurisdiction. Be sure to familiarize yourself with drug use, possession and trafficking laws at both the federal, state, and local level where you live.

The full disclaimer may be found at the end of this book.

YOUR FREE GIFT

Thanks for buying my book!

As a way of showing my appreciation, I would like to share with you a FREE Bonus Chapter:

"The 30 Habits of Self-Made Millionaires"

This bonus chapter is a great summary of everything that I've learned while interviewing self-made millionaires, as well as habits from my own life that have helped to make me successful.

To get your free copy, go here now:

https://www.trader.university/habits

HOW TO BECOME A SELF-MADE MILLIONAIRE

You are the average of the five people that you spend the most time with.

If you spend most of your time with criminals or lazy people, odds are that your life looks very much like theirs.

If you spend most of your time associating with millionaires, you too will most likely become a millionaire.

There's nothing magical about this.

It's simply a product of the law of averages and human susceptibility to influence.

And yet not everyone is lucky enough to be able to rub shoulders with millionaires every day.

I've been very lucky in my life.

My parents sent me to the same elite private high school that Bill Gates attended.

I was able to use this education as a spring board to get an undergraduate degree from Stanford University, and then a Ph.D. from UC-Berkeley.

It was at Stanford that I met Peter Thiel-- founder of PayPal, early Facebook investor, and now a billionaire.

After graduate school, Peter hired me to work at his multi-billion dollar hedge fund.

After that, I ran my own hedge fund.

I'm now retired from the money management business.

Today I run www.trader.university, where I teach both traders and investors how to make money in stocks, options, futures, and crypto.

I've been skilled (or lucky) enough to have one success after another.

And yet it's important to note that I don't consider myself a self-made millionaire.

I've had a lot of help along the way.

Without my wife, my children, my parents and my brother,

my friends, my teachers, and other mentors, I would never be where I am today.

Unfortunately, not everyone can launch their careers by attending Stanford University like I did.

In fact, I'm pretty certain I couldn't get into Stanford today.

So we're faced with a dilemma.

To become a millionaire, you need to hang out with other millionaires.

And yet it's difficult to hang out with other millionaires, if you are not a millionaire yourself.

It's a classic catch-22.

My solution is this book.

I've interviewed ordinary people who became self-made millionaires.

None of them inherited their wealth.

Instead, each of them earned every penny of it.

For this book, I won't be interviewing Peter Thiel, or any of the other professional hedge fund managers or Silicon Valley founders and investors that I know.

Those will have to wait for a later book.

For this book, I wanted to focus on ordinary people who became millionaires.

These are people who worked hard, but also worked smart.

All of them have another thing in common:

They are readers of my books on trading and investing.

I'm blessed to have been able to interview them.

One of the best things about writing and publishing books is all of the interesting people who contact you.

The self-made millionaires in this book are all voracious readers.

Even after making millions, they have never stopped reading and learning.

I'm grateful to them for having agreed to do these interviews with me.

By sharing their different paths to wealth, they are going to help a lot of people who read their stories.

That being said, all of them are private individuals who are not looking for publicity.

For this reason, I've omitted their names, and changed some identifying details to protect their privacy.

Even so, you are still going to get to "hang out" with them by reading these interviews.

Reading this book will change your perspective on life, business, and money.

Take out a pen and paper, and take some notes.

Absorb the morning routines, business hacks, investing strategies, and life philosophies that you will encounter.

Most of all, get inspired.

If they could do this, so can you.

In the 21st century, anyone can become a millionaire.

All it takes is some hard work and the right road map.

Now it's time to turn the page, and start learning from these self-made millionaires.

2

THE BIOHACKER

Tell us a little bit about your early life.

There's not much to say of interest. I grew up in Southern California in a home with loving parents. I spent way too much time hanging out on the beach and wasting time with my friends. I was a B student in high school and college, and got a boring job right out of college.

I was always a very passive person. I would date the first girl who showed an interest in me. I went to work for the first place that offered me a job. At work, I showed little to no initiative. I answered emails, returned phone calls, and put out fires as they occurred. I had no vision for the future and no appreciation for the present.

I think there's something about SoCal's nice weather that

lulls you into a state of inertia and numbness. To be honest with you, I really don't like to talk about this part of my life. Looking back on it, I don't even recognize this person as myself. He seems so foreign to me. He's definitely a loser.

Doesn't it seem a little harsh to judge your former self that way?

It might seem that way, but you have to understand where I am now. It's like I am a completely new organism, living a galaxy away from where I was before.

How is that?

Let's put it this way: I'm rich, I'm in amazing physical shape, I never get sick, I date only gorgeous women, and my knowledge is increasing exponentially every day.

I'm able to speed-read 3-4 books every day and quickly incorporate their contents into what I already know. I can talk or write at a very high level about world history, behavioral economics, nutrition, finance, physics, biochemistry, evolutionary psychology, nootropic drugs, and many other topics.

I've learned three new instruments in the last 12 months. I can sit in with any rock or jazz band and play pretty much anything. I can cook a gourmet French dinner on command. I can now also speak French and Russian fluently.

It's an amazing positive feedback loop that I've been in since 2011. I like to call it "better living through chemistry."

What kicked off this positive feedback loop?

In 2011, I went to see the movie "Limitless." It's about a struggling writer who discovers a smart drug (called NZT-48) that allows his mind to function at a superhuman level. He becomes able to learn foreign languages on the fly. He can remember everything that he has ever experienced or read, and then synthesize those memories to optimize his actions in the present. His enhanced IQ and superior powers of analysis allow him to go from being a loser with writer's block to a financial prodigy who operates at the highest echelons of power.

When I emerged from that movie theater into the broad daylight, I was a different person. I was like Saul on the road to Damascus. I was awake, I was energized, and I had been given a purpose for the first time in my life. It had never occurred to me before that life could be lived at such a high level. Before that, I had always lived at the low level of expectations that American society sets for us. Going to public school or watching TV is certainly not going to make you ambitious. All of the messages that you get from your teachers and from celebrities are wrong.

So what did you do next?

When I got home from the movie, the first thing that I did was to go online to try to find a smart drug just like NZT-48.

Not surprisingly, it didn't exist. That movie was science fiction after all.

I did, however, find a drug called Adderall. Adderall was originally designed to treat people with ADHD. It was later discovered by college students and Silicon Valley coders who use it as a productivity tool. I never used it in college myself, but knew other students who did.

This time I was ready to try it. So I did a little online research and found a local doctor who was well-known for prescribing Adderall to anyone who came to him. I brought the pills home after work, popped a couple, then wondered what to do next. Since I was experimenting with my own personal chemistry, I decided that it was appropriate to take a look at my old chemistry textbook from high school.

At first I didn't feel anything. I didn't feel especially happy or high. But then I noticed that I was actually reading the chemistry textbook, and enjoying it. This was the same text-book that had bored me to tears in the past. All of the concepts were now making perfect sense. I began to see how elegant the periodic table actually was. Stoichiometry made perfect sense. Acid-base reactions were positively cool.

When I finally looked up at the clock, it was 2 am. I had been reading that chemistry book since 7 pm, and enjoying every minute of it.

That was when I realized that my life was about to change.

For the next 3 months, I spent all of my evenings and weekends reading books while hopped up on Adderall. Since I wanted to become rich, I read the biographies of Warren Buffett, Sam Walton, Richard Branson, Ted Turner, and other successful businessmen that I had never paid much attention to before.

I also discovered Quora and Reddit and went down many rabbit holes on subjects as diverse as physics, economics, and the ancestral health movement. MarksDailyApple.com is a great place to learn about the paleo diet and ancestral health, and I devoured everything that Mark Sisson wrote.

I was learning an amazing amount about optimal health, but ironically my own health began to suffer from all of the Adderall that I was taking. I wasn't sleeping well, and I began to have daily panic attacks. Adderall is basically an amphetamine cocktail, so this isn't surprising. I quickly realized that I was going to end up really hurting myself if I didn't change my life style. The only problem was that I had become addicted not only to the Adderall, but also to the accelerated learning that it made possible.

But I had learned a major lesson in the process that has stuck with me every since:

If you can change your biochemistry, you can change your life.

At this point in my independent studies, I had learned

enough about human health to realize that it was extremely important to optimize sleep, nutrition, and exercise in order to optimize biochemistry. Just think how your mental state changes if you have not slept well, or have binged on sugar, or have watched 6 hours of TV. You're a different person. Biochemistry is everything. That's not something that parents or the high schools teach.

So I came up with a plan. I would slowly reduce my dosage of Adderall, until I was completely off the drug. At the same time, I would begin to optimize my sleep. That seemed to be the central pillar of good health. And I knew that on the days when I was well-rested, my powers of concentration were much better, my productivity was much higher, and I was much less tempted by junk food and TV binges.

So I bought a good sleep mask and blackout shades to make sure that my bedroom was completely dark. Any stray light in your bedroom will inhibit the secretion of melatonin and interfere with the quality of your sleep. I made sure that my bedroom was always 65 degrees Fahrenheit at night. I also bought a big bag of earplugs. Even sounds that don't wake you up can interfere with high quality delta sleep.

I stopped using all electronic devices like computers or phones 3-4 hours before bed, because of the negative effects of blue light on sleep.

I gave up all alcohol consumption (which interferes with

good sleep), stopped eating at least 4 hours before bedtime, made sure that I never exercised or drank caffeine after noon, and tried to always go to bed and wake up at the same time.

I still go to bed at 9 pm every night and wake up naturally without an alarm at about 6 am. This gives me at least 8 hours of quality sleep.

Many people think that sleeping is a waste of time. They couldn't be more wrong. It's one of my superpowers.

Getting better sleep (especially delta or deep sleep) helped me to reform my diet as well. I gave up sugar in all of its forms, and tried to move my diet more towards the kinds of foods that my great-grandparents ate. Lots of organic vegetables grown in nutrient-rich soils, and high-quality grass-fed dairy and beef. No sugar, no gluten, and definitely no soybean, corn, or cottonseed oils.

At this point, I discovered that I work best when I eat only once a day. When I wake up, I will have some coffee or other plant medicines that help me to study. But I will hold off on eating until about 2 pm or 3 pm, when I have my only meal of the day. I find that I concentrate better on an empty stomach. It's also the most natural way to incorporate intermittent fasting into your lifestyle.

A high quality diet and ample sleep led me naturally to the third pillar: exercise. I got a gym membership, and began to lift weights regularly, focusing especially on exercises that activate the biggest muscles in the body like the quads and the glutes. I made sure that I made plenty of time for hikes and long jogs on the beach as well.

Up until this point, I was focused strictly on getting back to being a human being. Most modern people do not sleep, eat, or exercise in any way that would be recognizable to our ancestors.

What were the next steps that you took?

Now that I had become a human being again, it was time to focus on becoming superhuman. I hadn't forgotten about the benefits of Adderall. I wanted to find a more natural way to get back to that super-productive mental space.

So I began to study and experiment with the plant medicines that have been used over thousands of years by great civilizations: coffee, cannabis, yerba mate, ginseng, gingko biloba, bacopa monnieri (Brahmi). Over the years, I have found coffee and cannabis to be the most useful for my practices.

Doesn't the regular use of marijuana make you lazy and unmotivated?

Cannabis is what some people have called a non-specific amplifier. If you are already lazy, it will make you more lazy. If you are already ambitious, it will amplify your ambition. So much depends on the set and setting and your reasons for using cannabis. If you want to use it to numb yourself and drop out, the plant will allow that. If you want to use it as a self-enhancement tool, the plant will also allow that.

Can you give us an example?

Have you ever heard of a "hippie speedball"? It's basically when you go for a 20-minute jog, and then come back and drink a cup of coffee and have a few hits of a nice high-pinene, high-limonene sativa. It's the perfect recipe for tricking your brain into entering a state of "flow," where all things become possible. It allows me to read or write for literally 5 hours on end without any distractions.

Again, none of these are recommendations for anyone else. I'm just telling you what works for me. Don't use drugs that are illegal where you live. It does make sense, however, to do the research and see how these plant medicines have been used by great civilizations. Then maybe move somewhere where they are legal.

Coffee was illegal in both Mecca and Sweden at various points. It was eventually legalized, because how are you ever going to compete with people who drink coffee when you don't? It's a structural advantage for a civilization to allow both coffee and cannabis.

Anything else?

Yes, I also take Metformin every day. It's a prescription drug that has traditionally been used to treat Type 2 diabetes, but which is currently being explored by researchers as an anti-aging drug. I know 2 billionaires who are not diabetic, but who take Metformin every day for this reason.

I also take maca root, which is great for libido and energy, as well as lion's mane mushroom, which is great for mental focus as well as immune system health.

I take a few other prescription drugs that I rather not speak about, because these are off-label uses. They might eventually kill me, but I doubt it. It's more likely that they will massively increase my life span. Some of them have already made me smarter, as demonstrated by IQ tests that I have taken.

Why take so many risks?

It all boils down to this: the longer you live, and the more productive you are, the more you can accomplish. Time is the most valuable commodity that you have. Attention is our second most valuable commodity. By maximizing both, you can massively increase your daily and lifetime productivity.

Do you have any advice to readers who want to follow a similar path?

Start slow and easy. I'm taking risks which the average person should definitely not take. If you are still working a boring job, you can try to buy yourself some time to learn a new skill. Start drinking yerba mate on the weekends, and use that time to learn a new skill. Skip Netflix and social media for 6 months, and you'll be surprised by what you can accomplish.

And then use the new skills that you have acquired to bootstrap yourself to a higher level, both intellectually and financially.

Rich and educated people like to be around other rich and educated and interesting people. If you're not yet rich, at least you can become more educated and interesting. First optimize your sleep, diet, and exercise, and then go from there.

How did you first become a millionaire?

I tried a number of online businesses without success. My first breakthrough was when I built an online marketing tool that helps e-commerce companies to grow their sales. I basically realized after failing a number of times that I needed to work backwards from the problem to the solution. If you can create a tool that creates more value for someone's business than they spend on the tool, it becomes quite easy to sell that tool.

In the process of selling that tool, I became friends with a number of prominent founders in Silicon Valley who have allowed me to invest in their start-ups. Most of my net worth has come from investing in these friends' companies. A lot of

Silicon Valley founders also share my interest in biohacking. Moving to the Bay Area was the best thing that I ever did. If you want to do tech and biohacking, it's the only place to be.

These days, most of my investments are on auto-pilot. In addition to investing in startups directly, I'm also invested in VC funds, hedge funds, and a lot of commercial real estate. It's a bit of a barbell strategy. My commercial real estate portfolio is fairly conservative, and is skewed towards senior housing, skilled nursing facilities, and other healthcare properties. I think these investments will continue to do well with the aging population as a tail-wind. My other investments are more speculative, with a much higher reward and risk profile.

I've moved almost everything to autopilot in order to enable me to continue my process of learning without interruption. I get up early, and spend most of my day reading. I never check the markets or waste my time on social media. I've become a learning machine.

Most of my research these days is focused on life extension, including how to upgrade the human body using wearables, implants, microchips, and other modifications. I am also working closely with a few transhumanist start-ups to help to push forward this melding of man and machine.

My ultimate goal is to defeat death, or at least to delay it for as long as possible.

How long do you expect to live?

I'm not just trying to increase my life span by 15%. I'm trying to jump on and ride the singularity. In 200,000 years from now, I would like to be the ruler of a great new civilization that covers an entire galaxy. At that point, I will probably be some mixture of consciousness and hardware that is difficult to define at the moment. Peter Thiel says that you should endeavor to compete in arenas where there is very little competition. At the present time, I don't think I have any competitors, except perhaps people like Elon Musk or Peter Thiel. I think that the total addressable market of the universe is large enough for us three to split.

A lot of my readers are going to say that you are delusional.

I might be. It's certainly possible. There's a fine line between being the visionary and being the madman. The Church of England bishop Francis Godwin wrote a book ("The Man in the Moone") about traveling to the moon in 1638 that was widely considered delusional and endlessly parodied. Today moon travel has left the realm of fiction and entered the realm of science. And yet people still constantly underestimate how far science and technological advances can take us.

We live in a culture that tells us that "you can make all of your dreams come true." At the same time, it fails to encourage much ambition in formulating those dreams. If you can make all of your dreams come true, then why just settle for getting a "dream job"? That's a pretty limited goal.

Western civilization at its best has always had lofty goals. We're at our best when we're looking up at the stars and making plans. That's why I admire people like Elon Musk who never tire of saying that we need to become a space-faring civilization.

In my experience, there are very few people in this world who prioritize learning and achievement over self-indulgent activities like collecting material possessions, sex, fancy food, drugs and alcohol, etc.

I'm not interested in luxuries. For me, money is just a stepping stone that I can use to get to a higher level of existence. It's important not to idolize money too much. It's simply a tool to get you from point A to point B. If you have a lot of it and use it wisely, you might be able to get from point A to point X, or beyond. If you're smart and rich enough, you might even be able to live forever.

Any final thoughts for our readers?

There's a split that's happening in our world. There is a new super species of humans that is splitting off from regular humans. These new super-humans understand the power of biohacking to increase productivity. They take smart drugs, and they know how to optimize sleep, nutrition, and exercise. As a result, they always beat the competition.

Regular humans have no idea how far they are being left behind.

Imagine that you are racing against the cyclist Lance Armstrong. You work out every day religiously. Lance does too. But he is also doing blood transfusions, blood doping, injecting himself with testosterone and other performance-enhancing drugs. You're not doing those extra things, so he beats you in every race.

Since he is winning every race, he is getting more and more wealthy. Now he can afford the best doctors, consultants, and the most expensive and powerful performance-enhancing drugs. You don't even know these drugs exist, and even if you did, you wouldn't be able to afford them. So you never catch up to Lance.

Now let's turn to the real world of health and wealth and business. What Lance did was against the rules of the game. But in the real world, there are no rules against biohacking. So you can use biohacking to optimize your physical and mental faculties.

Your competition needs more sleep, but you don't. You're also always in a good mood. You've mastered the art of sales and persuasion and you use it in business and dating all the time. You are always charming, persuasive, and preternaturally informed. You get access to the best VC deals.

And you also get access to the most beautiful and intelligent women. Now you are making babies and using CRISPR to edit their genes so that they are smarter and taller and better-looking than anyone else.

You and your partner can afford to give your kids private tutors, and to spike their drinks with smart drugs. Even without that, you are able to donate the $10 million that automatically gets your kid into Harvard or Stanford.

Evolution is now taking place at an accelerated rate, aided by technology. Regular humans are being left behind and they don't even know it. They are wasting their time on Netflix and Facebook, while we super-humans are taking over the world. Their children will be working for my children. I'd like for them to at least know the game that is being played.

Thanks for taking the time to talk with me today.

3

MAKING MONEY WITH TOILETS
AND BEER

Tell us a little bit about your early life.

I was born in 1960 in the Bay Area, where I've lived ever since. My father was a plumber, and I decided to follow him into the trade. I've always been good with my hands, and not afraid of a little dirt. It's not glamorous work, but I enjoy the freedom of being my own boss.

Did you go to college?

I did not. I went straight into plumbing after high school.

Do you focus on residential or commercial plumbing?

I only do residential plumbing. I'm a one-man shop. No employees, no business location. Besides my plumbing tools, all I need is a cell phone, an old van, and a good Yelp listing. I don't even really need Yelp, since most of my business is word of mouth at this point. Being a plumber is a great business, because you don't need a lot of assets (or business loans) to start your business.

Some of my readers might be surprised to learn that you are a millionaire. There are lots of people with MBA's and law degrees that are not millionaires.

Like I said, there's nothing glamorous about what I do. You don't need a 120 IQ to install a toilet or unplug a sink. The good news is that robots haven't put me out of a job yet. When someone calls me on a Sunday night with a flooded toilet, I'm as important to them as a trusted attorney or tax adviser.

What do you charge?

$150/hour plus materials. I could probably charge more, since folks are usually desperate when they call me. But that's about the going rate.

How many hours do you work per week?

I work about 30 hours per week on average, not counting time spent in traffic.

So that's about $18,000/month before taxes?

Yes.

That's incredible. You're basically making the same amount of money as a Google engineer.

Yes, but without the stock options, of course. Your readers need to realize that the Bay Area is a very expensive place to live these days. The median price of a home in my area is over $1.5 million, and that's for a pretty crappy house. I'm lucky to have bought my house in the 1980's before tech took off.

So I imagine that your house has helped to make you a millionaire.

Yes, I have more than a millionaire dollars in equity in my house. But that's only a part of the story.

Really?

I've been a beer drinker all of my life. It's my only vice, though I wish I exercised more. Ironically, it's my beer habit that has made me more money than anything else. I've been drinking Sam Adams beer for as long as I can remember. It's still my favorite beer.

Well, in 1995, I began to see announcements on Sam Adams six-packs that the company was going to sell shares to the public. There was a toll-free number that you could call to get 33 shares of stock at $15 each. So I immediately called the number and purchased my $495 worth of the stock. A few months later when the official IPO happened, those shares that I had bought at 15 were trading in the high 20's. The stock got as high as 33 before crashing all the way down to 6.50 by the late 1990's. The internet boom was in full swing, and nobody wanted shares of old economy companies like brewers.

I had a different opinion. I knew that the Boston Beer Company (SAM) made the best microbrew beer in the world. I drank a few bottles of Sam Adams every night, and so was constantly reminded of this. And so I decided to start adding to my position in SAM by using all of my available cash to buy more shares. I used all of the available profits from my plumbing business, after paying our household expenses, to buy more shares of SAM. On the 15th of every month since 1998, I've been buying shares of SAM. Those same shares that I paid between 6.50 and 10 for in 1998 are now worth over 300 per share. I'm a multi-millionaire today because of SAM.

Have you ever sold any of your shares?

I sold some to pay for my children's college education, but I still own most of my shares. Literally millions of dollars worth. My wife keeps telling me that I should sell the whole thing and put the cash into a safe CD. I might do that one of these days, but at this point I'm emotionally attached to them. I love the beer, and I love the company that makes it.

We often hear that when investing you should not put all of your eggs in one basket. Are you guilty of this?

I think that the second half of that proverb is that if you do put all of your eggs in one basket, make sure you watch that basket closely, or something to that effect. I'm definitely guilty of not diversifying. But I've also heard from folks like Warren Buffett that you can only get huge returns by owning just a few stocks. If you own the 500 stocks in the S&P 500, your results will just be average.

I think that everyone has to decide for themselves what they are comfortable with. I have read every annual report that SAM ever put out, so I am definitely watching my basket very closely.

Are you married?

Yes, I am married with 2 grown children. One works for Google, and the other works for Facebook. I'm not a bit sorry that they haven't followed me into my profession.

Is there anything about your morning routine that you would like to share?

Now that my children are all grown up, I like to wake up slowly in the morning. The Bay Area is expensive, but the weather is just perfect here. I usually have a leisurely breakfast sitting at an outside table in the sun. I find that 20 minutes of early morning sunlight and fresh air really helps me to wake up and feel good about starting the day.

Any advice for high school or college students?

Don't be afraid to go into the trades. Our country has a shortage of craftsmen, plumbers, electricians, repair men, etc. College isn't for everyone. Be realistic about student loans and what you are going to study in college. Will you really be able to pay off those loans, which will otherwise stick with you for life?

Any other advice?

Invest in what you know. If you are regularly spending money on something, why not get some of that money back from the company in the form of dividends and capital gains? My life would be very different today if I had never invested in the Boston Beer Company. Also make sure that you find a good spouse who shares your financial and personal values. Take each day as it comes, and appreciate the small things. Life just flies by, so take the time to appreciate the little moments.

Thanks for taking the time to talk with me today.

4

THE KING OF FORECLOSURES

Tell us a little bit about your early life.

I was born in 1981 in Citrus Heights, a sleepy suburb of Sacramento, CA. I had a pretty typical American childhood. During the summer, I'd leave the house after breakfast and not return until sunset. My friends and I rode our bikes everywhere. We climbed trees, splashed around in streams, and probably threw a few eggs at cars passing by. I'm not proud of that last thing. I think these were the years that the Golden State Killer was on the loose, but my parents must not have been reading the newspapers.

After high school, I went to a local community college and studied real estate. During the summers, I worked for a couple of real estate agents as basically an errand boy. Neither of these agents were successful. It was at this time that I learned that every real estate office usually has just one or two high producers who bring in most of the business. The agents that I worked for were lucky to sell 10 houses every year, while the high producer in the office was selling over 100 houses per year.

Did you end up getting a job in real estate after college?

I had not been thrilled with my experiences in real estate up to that point, so I decided to look elsewhere. I ended up going to work for a giant health insurance company for the next 8 years. It was your typical white-collar, paper-pusher job. Workdays were boring, but I never had to bring home any work to ruin my evenings or weekends.

Are you still with the same company?

No, I am not. My first 5 years with the company were fine. Boring, but pretty easy. Then sometime around my 27th birthday, I began to get restless. It was almost as if I had been sleep-walking my entire life-- and then one day I suddenly woke up. I looked around at my life and wondered how I had put up with it for so long. It wasn't exactly a spiritual awakening, but it like I was suddenly seeing my life with new eyes. I began to hate my cubicle, the constant ringing of the phone, the smell of my boss's bad coffee breath. It's strange because I had been pretty content up until that point.

So did you quit?

I couldn't afford to quit, but I definitely began to plan my escape. I began to read books about real estate again, to try to bring back what I had learned in college. Then the Great Financial Crisis of 2008-2009 hit, and I was just focused on not losing my job.

Did you own or rent at the time?

I had never had the savings or the desire to own a house. I liked the convenience of living in an apartment complex. I had good friends in the complex, and enjoyed the small weight room and the pool.

Then in late 2011 and early 2012, I began to notice more for-sale signs in my neighborhood than I had ever seen before. Housing prices had peaked in 2006 during the great housing bubble and had been going down ever since. Lots of people had their homes foreclosed on. By 2011 and 2012, the banks had taken control of these homes and were dumping them on the market.

It was about this time that I discovered Redfin.com. I still remember the day that I searched for tenant-occupied homes. Basically, you can search for single family homes, and then put "renter" or "tenant" in the keyword section. That gave me a list of homes for sale that had a tenant living in the house. I began to call real estate agents to see how much these tenants were each paying in rent, and whether they had plans to stay.

I was very surprised to learn that many of these tenants had been living for years at the same property and always paying their rent on time. What surprised me more were the rental yields.

Can you explain the concept of rental yield?

Yes, let me explain it by discussing one of those houses that I ended up buying. It was on the market for $95,000 and I ended up paying $89,000. It was a 3 bedroom, 2 bathroom house, and the tenants were paying $1,000 per month. That's $12,000 per year. Now take that $12,000 and divide it by my purchase price of $89,000 and you get 13.48%. That's called the gross rental yield, since it doesn't include other expenses that a landlord usually has to pay. Fortunately these tenants paid all of the utilities, so I was only left with having to pay property taxes and insurance, which subtracted about 2.50% from that yield.

So I was basically making about 11% cash on cash on that house. Now this is amazing when you realize that savings accounts at the time were paying about 1%, if you were lucky. I was making 11 times that, and the only risk was that my tenants stopped paying their rent.

Where did you get the cash to buy that house?

That is the best part. At the time, I had only about $50,000 in savings, which wasn't enough to even buy one house.

Were you able to take out a mortgage to buy the house?

I probably would have been able to borrow some money from a bank, but the real problem was that these foreclosed houses were all-cash deals. The banks were offering the foreclosed houses at fire-sale prices, but they wanted to be paid in cash. If you didn't pay cash, there was always another real estate investor who would come in and pay cash and take the home away from you.

So where did you get the remaining $34,000 to buy that house?

As it ended up, I did not use a single penny of my own money to buy that house. Some of my friends and co-workers had been complaining that they were only making 1% in their savings accounts. Suddenly it occurred to me that I could borrow money from them, pay them 5% interest per year, and still have a lot of cash flow left over.

So I borrowed $89,000 from them, and bought the house for all-cash. We did a quick property inspection, and were able to close the deal in a week, since it was all-cash.

After property taxes and insurance, I was being paid about $9,800 per year in rent by the tenants. I hired a property management company, which took 10% of that-- $980. I set aside another $1,000 for future repairs and maintenance bills, so that left me with cash flow of $7,820 per year.

Now I had to pay my friends and coworkers 5% a year on that $89,000, or $4,450.

That still left me with annual cash flow of $3,370. The amazing thing is that I was being paid to own this house.

That was early 2012. Over the years, I was able to increase the rent every year after that, so my annual cash flow also went up.

But the real magic happened with real estate prices recovering. In mid 2017, I was able to sell that same house for about $289,000 after commissions.

I paid back my friends and coworkers the $89,000 that I had borrowed. That still left me with $200,000 in profits and I had never had to risk a penny of my own money. You can see why real estate has minted so many new millionaires. There's no other market that let's you trade with someone else's money like that.

How many houses did you end up buying?

I ended up buying 20 foreclosed single family homes. I would have bought more, but housing prices began to move up quickly by the end of 2012, as lots of hedge funds and other institutional investors began to enter the market.

Some of the houses that I bought ended up having serious problems like mold or damaged foundations that the property inspections had missed. But even including these, I was able to make a lot of money. A rising market really helps to bail you out of your mistakes.

All in all, I was able to net over $2 million after taxes by the end of 2017 when I sold the last of those 20 houses.

So you were basically arbitraging the spread between what you could borrow money at, and the net rental yield?

Yes. In addition to borrowing money from friends, coworkers, and family at around 5%, I also borrowed money from what are called "hard money lenders." They charged closer to 8-10% interest rates. My only goal was for my portfolio of houses to be cash flow neutral (i.e. not losing any money) overall. That way I could hold on to these houses with no out-of-pocket costs, and just wait for them to appreciate.

Do you still work for that big health insurance company?

No, I quit in 2017 after I began to sell off my houses.

How do you spend your time these days?

I got married in 2015, and my wife and I now have 2 beautiful young children. I'm spending all of my time with my wife and kids, and also doing some serious golfing. In the meantime, I'm waiting for the next housing collapse, whether it's in California or elsewhere. This time around I have both the cash and the expertise to really profit.

Thanks for taking the time to talk with me today.

5

FREE MONEY FROM THE UNIVERSE

Tell us a little bit about your early life.

I was born in Palo Alto and attended Palo Alto High School. I then went up the street to Stanford, and got a degree in computer science.

What was your first job after graduation?

It was not at all what I expected. Those who are familiar with the Silicon Valley of today may have a difficult time visualizing how depressed the area was at that time. In the early 1990's when I graduated, the U.S. was in a recession. Silicon Valley was also in a recession. The hardware business had been slowing down, and the Internet had not yet really begun. The Netscape IPO was still a few years away.

When I graduated, there were not a lot of good software jobs around. Or at least no one wanted to hire me. I probably did not have the best attitude. I was cocky and smart, and clearly did not respect authority.

Had you always been like that?

Actually, no. I was always a straight A student, and school came very naturally to me. I had been programming since 5th grade on my own, so I found the computer science curriculum at Stanford to be quite easy. I had a lot of free time on my hands in college. And it being California, it was probably inevitable that I would spend some of that time experimenting with recreational drugs.

What drugs did you try?

I was not your normal college druggie, just wanting to get drunk or high. In high school, I had read Aldous Huxley's Doors of Perception about his personal experimentation with mescaline, a psychedelic drug derived from the peyote cactus. Huxley was an English intellectual and a brilliant writer as well. The book contains amazing descriptions of Huxley's experience on psychedelics. I wanted to experience the same thing first hand. I wasn't able to find mescaline on the Stanford campus, but I did find "magic mushrooms" whose active ingredient was a similar psychedelic called psilocybin.

I'll never forget my first experience after ingesting these magic mushrooms. Time seemed to stop, all of the colors in the dorm room began to glow, and the music that I was listening to exploded with transcendental beauty. Even everyday items like my bed and desk shimmered like mystical objects. And I could actively manipulate my external environment. Just by thinking about it, I could turn my desk from brown to bright blue. I could make the rock music sound like classical music. My mind was actively authoring reality.

Now anyone who has ever taken a psychedelic knows that it is very difficult to build a bridge from that experience and connect it to our everyday experience of life. That's why we have the mental category of "weird drug experiences from college." What do drug experiences have to do with the reality of living in the real world and making money?

It turns out, in my case, quite a lot. What I realized while high on psychedelics is that reality is not solid. It is infinitely malleable. In fact, there is probably no objective reality out there. Or if there is one, it's not something that we have ready access to. There's only the subjective version of reality that emanates from our minds. We create reality with our thoughts.

Now you have to understand that I'm not a religious person. I'm not talking spiritual mumbo-jumbo here. I mean what I am saying quite literally: we can literally change reality with our minds. In fact, I do it all the time. All I need to do is to focus on a specific outcome, and it usually happens.

Here's how I do it. I take out a clean sheet of paper, and write down what I want 30 times every morning before breakfast. So, for example: "I will date so and so the Stanford cheerleader." I will write that down every day by hand using paper and ink. It feels a little silly doing it, but it actually works about 85% of the time. For example, I actually ended up dating that Stanford cheerleader, and I can assure you that she was way out of my league. My friends never stopped reminding me of that.

Now the first couple of times this technique worked, I was pretty sure that it was a coincidence. So I decided to do something crazy. Why not use the same technique to make a boatload of money? That would solve most of my problems at the time. And since this was all fantasy and make-believe after all, why not aim for $10 million, instead of just $100,000? So every morning before breakfast, I began to write down "I will make $10 million in the next 2 years" thirty times.

Before I tell you what happened, let me tell you why I think this technique works. Now you are really going to think that I am weird.

I'm afraid my readers have already pigeonholed you as a druggie, so I'm not sure if you can make things worse.

Ha! Well, here it goes. I am convinced that we are all living in a software simulation.

What do you mean?

I mean that you and I are literally zeros and ones in a software program. We only exist as characters in a virtual world.

What makes you think that?

Well, the main reason I think that is that I seem to be able to get whatever I want, simply by willing it to happen. That is not how the real world should work. That is more how video games work.

But there is a probabilistic argument as well. We can assume that whenever a civilization reaches a certain advanced point in technology, it becomes able to create software. Software makes it possible to create virtual worlds. Once you have one virtual world, it becomes possible to have new virtual worlds that have been programmed by the inhabitants of the first virtual world. This can go on ad infinitum, and is not limited by real world constraints. In fact, new virtual worlds might arise extremely quickly within virtual worlds.

If we look at the world that we inhabit, there is a much greater probability that we are living in one of these virtual worlds (since there can be so many of them), than that we are living in the original physical real world.

There is simply a much higher probability that we are living in a software simulation, than that we are living in the original real world that created the first software. If you were a betting man, you would want to bet in such a way so as to have the probabilities on your side.

Isn't it also possible that you are mentally ill, because of your previous drug use?

Yes, it is certainly possible. But here's the strange thing. There's really no way to tell the difference. Now that you have heard about my software simulation hypothesis, you are going to have trouble viewing the world in the same way that you always have. I might be mentally ill, but my hypothesis could still be true.

You can test the hypothesis yourself by trying to use your will to change your experience of reality. Every morning for 3 months, write down something that you want to happen 30 times, and see what happens. You have only your time, ink, and paper to lose. It's a fairly easy way to test the hypothesis for yourself. I see the world as a software simulation, and so I live my life accordingly. I'm now extremely rich, and I'm being interviewed by you for your book, so life has been good to me in this particular simulation.

Is there any other evidence for your hypothesis?

Yes, funny you should ask. Let's think about this for a second. If you were creating your own software simulation, it would probably have to include two very important characteristics, in order to be effective.

First, you could not allow the inhabitants of your simulation to travel to the edge of your simulation. If they did, they would quickly realize that they were living in a simulation. As it turns out, we are not able to get to the edge of our universe. We are constrained by the speed of light, and by a constantly expanding universe. How convenient!

Second, you could not allow the inhabitants of your simulation to see what their world was made out of. If they did, they would quickly realize that it was constructed purely of bits and bytes. Then they would get extremely mad at you. Now as it turns out, as we try to investigate what our universe is made out of, we run into similar problems. Quantum weirdness takes over, and it becomes impossible to observe the basic building blocks of our universe. Again, how convenient!

Both of these points are good evidence that we currently inhabit a software simulation.

Steve Jobs was famous for his "reality distortion field." Do you think he was exploiting an understanding of reality that is similar to your own?

Steve Jobs is no longer with us, and even if he were, I would be unable to read his mind. That being said, I think that Steve Jobs is one of a few public figures who seemed to possess voodoo powers that allowed him to accomplish whatever he wanted. From the outside, it appears that he was able to bend reality. It is interesting that before he became an entrepreneur and CEO, Jobs spent many years dropping acid, meditating, and following Indian gurus. Perhaps it was these experiences that taught him how to manipulate the simulation. His results were probably better than if he had gone to biz school.

Any other public figures that come to mind?

Certainly Elon Musk. His ability to bend reality is extraordinary. And then, though it pains me to say it, there is Donald Trump. His powers are extraordinary, though I despise many of his views. There is no doubt in my mind that he understands these things, even if it is just at an intuitive level.

So far, we've talked about drugs and how to prosper in a software simulation. Were you able to parlay this knowledge into actually becoming a millionaire?

Yes, I was. Now for most people, trading stocks is considered a difficult activity. People expect to lose money (or even desire to lose money at a deep unconscious level), and so it's no surprise that most of them do.

My view of trading is quite different. I know that I inhabit a simulation, and so I can "program" the simulation to give me money whenever I need it. This makes trading quite easy for me, and it allowed me to become a millionaire in my 20's.

Shortly after I started writing "I will make $10 million in the next 2 years," I came across Jack Schwager's interviews with traders in <u>Market Wizards</u>. The interview with Ed Seykota had a big influence on me. Ed was basically a trend-follower, who bought breakouts and then tried to hold on to his winners and dump his losers. But it was his philosophy that had an even bigger impact on my trading. In that interview, Seykota says that "Everybody gets what they want out of the market. Some people like to lose, so they win big by losing money."

When I read this interview, I was already a big believer that the universe was designed to give us what we wanted. Seykota's comment really solidified it for me. In the same book, there is an interview with Michael Marcus, who turned $30,000 into $80 million. In fact, there are interviews with 15 other traders who accomplished similarly amazing things in the futures market and the stock market.

Reading this book, I realized that most of the traders were following a similar trend-following methodology. Buy things that are going up in price, sell things that are going down in price. Hold on to things that are going up, and dump things that are going down. This is the kind of simple rule that you would expect from a software simulation.

So I opened up an account at Datek, one of the early online discount brokers.

What year was this?

1997. I was living in Silicon Valley, so I naturally gravitated to the tech stocks that all of my computer science friends from school were talking about. But I had an edge over them. My friends thought that the fundamentals mattered. They had intricate opinions about whether Dell or Compaq made better computers, or whether Netscape or another company would win the browser wars. They thought that Amazon was a joke when it came public with a $500 million valuation as a low-margin bookstore.

I had opinions about these things too, but I tried to keep my opinions out of my trading. I just bought stocks that went up, that were hitting new all-time highs. Then I held on to them until they closed below the 50-day or 200-day moving average. I kept it simple. I also juiced my returns by trading on margin, as well as buying calls on these same momentum stocks. A simple trend-following system like this made you 20-30x on your money just in Amazon, even without leverage. If I had had your trading books at the time, I think I would have done even better.

How much money did you start trading with?

I started with $10,000 in 1997, and had turned it into over $10 million after taxes by the time the market peaked in 2000. Once again, the simulation had given me what I asked for.

Did you use any other trading strategies besides trend-following?

Yes, but you could hardly call it a trading strategy, and it's unfortunately something that you can't do anymore. Once I had a few hundred thousand dollars, I was able to open up accounts with more mainstream Wall Street brokers like Goldman, UBS, Merrill, etc. At that time, if you traded a lot of shares, you could be given allocations in new IPO's.

The way it worked was this: trade 500,000 shares of stock and you'll get a piece of the latest new hot IPO— VA Linux or The Globe or whatever. So what I would do is just churn my account. I'd buy 10,000 shares of a stock that was trading sideways and then try to get out as quickly as possible at my breakeven cost, or at a slight profit in order to pay for the commission. Once I had traded enough shares, I would be given an allocation in the latest IPO. I would pay something like $40,000 for 2,000 shares of the latest IPO. When the stock opened the next day at $80, I would dump the stock for a quick $120,000 profit. It was crazy. It didn't last long, but I made a lot of money while it did.

Did you get badly hurt in the great bear market of 2000-2002?

No. I initially lost some money, but once the QQQ and SPY were trending below their 200-day moving averages, I moved completely to cash. I watched many other traders and friends try to "buy the dips" and get slaughtered in the process.

A lot of this sounds to me like you were just in the right place at the right time. Silicon Valley was a great place to be if you wanted to get rich in the late 1990's.

Yes, it's certainly possible. From the outside, it might just look like I was smart or lucky, or a combination of the two. As they say, luck favors the prepared mind. At the time, I had been reading lots of books about trading, as well as general books about business. If I hadn't been a voracious reader, I might never have come across Schwager's book.

So maybe it was just luck. But the strange thing is that I have been lucky my whole life. It hasn't stopped.

From the outside, you'll never know what really happened. The simulation is programmed in such a way so as to not compel belief from its inhabitants.

How do you spend your time these days, now that you're independently wealthy?

I now spend about half of my time learning new musical instruments. I can now play piano, guitar, violin, cello, trumpet, and drums. Many people think that it's difficult to learn a new musical instrument, because they have bad memories of piano lessons as a child. Nothing could be further from the truth. If you can drive a car and hold down a job, you can easily learn any musical instrument. It's actually quite easy, if you are an adult with an average IQ. And once you understand that it's just part of the software simulation, it becomes even easier.

I spend the other half of my time trading momentum stocks. The last two years have been absolutely amazing for momentum tech stocks, as you know. The simulation seems to have served up a repeat of the late 1990's. Trend-following has worked extremely well on NVDA, NFLX, AMZN, and lots of other tech names. I've made more money this time around than I did in the dot-com bubble.

Do you think it will all end badly again?

Yes, without a doubt. Our universe is filled with recycled plots, probably because the guy who programmed it believed in conserving computing resources. Or maybe he was just lazy. The recycled plots are everywhere. Empires rise and fall. Middle-age balding man buys a convertible and cheats on his wife with the nanny. The stock market melts up, and then crashes. These plots are pathetically simple. We've had a bull market for the past 9 years, and this one will end badly like all the rest of them did. The good news is that it won't come out of nowhere. I like your recent book on bear markets. As you point out in that book, we'll have lots of warning before a bear market hits, as the indices and individual stocks all fall below their 50 or 200-day moving averages and stay there.

Can you recommend some of your favorite books that might be helpful to younger readers?

Walter Isaacson's biography of Steve Jobs is fantastic. Jobs' ability to steer the software simulation is present on every page. I also love Scott Adams' How to Fail at Everything and Still Win Big and Win Bigly. I love his cartoons (Dilbert), but his books are even better. There is even an appendix to Win Bigly that discusses the simulation hypothesis. In How to Fail at Everything and Still Win Big, Scott Adams discusses what he calls the "affirmations" technique. It's the same pen and paper method that I used many years ago. As it turns out, many years ago, Scott Adams wrote "I, Scott Adams, will become a famous cartoonist." If you believe him (and I do), this technique enabled him to influence the software simulation and actually become a famous cartoonist. I wouldn't believe a word of it, if I hadn't used the same technique to make $10 million. Scott Adams and I are strangely connected in the simulation. We've definitely had some similar experiences, and we view the world pretty much the same.

Any parting thoughts?

You can actually make things happen in your life, simply by focusing on them, and by constantly bringing your thoughts back to them. You can call it magic, the power of positive thinking, "the secret," visualization technique, or the natural result of living in a software simulation. If you're a Wiccan, you can call it magic. I'm a computer science sort of guy, so I prefer the software simulation metaphor.

I don't know why it works, but it does.

The good news is that you don't even have to actually believe that it works.

You just need to have the discipline to write your wish down on a piece of paper 30 times every day for 3 months.

I'm sure this will turn out to be the craziest interview in your book.

If it makes your reader feel better, I would encourage him just to spend less money than he makes, and invest the balance in an index fund. That's really boring, but it will make you rich over 40 years.

But if you are impatient, as I am, just ask the universe to serve up what you want immediately.

You might just be surprised by what happens.

Thanks for taking the time to talk with me today.

6

THE EARLY RETIREES

How old were you when you retired?

My wife and I both retired in 2017, when we turned 35 years old.

How was this possible?

Too few people realize how easy it can be to retire early. All it takes is some good planning, some discipline, and most importantly some automation.

I got married right out of college at the age of 22. Very early on in our marriage, my wife and I made the commitment to save 50% of our after-tax income. This can be easier than it sounds if you can automate everything.

To begin with, we both maxed out our 401k's at work and made sure that we took full advantage of our employers' 401k matching programs. Our 401k's were always invested in index funds.

Next, we set up bi-monthly automatic transfers that swept 50% of our after-tax paychecks from our joint checking account to a brokerage account that we were not allowed to touch. So then we were forced to live on whatever was left over in our checking account until the next paycheck.

This kind of forced savings can be very helpful. It takes all of the decision making out of it. As my father used to always say, "Pay yourself first!"

Any other savings hacks that you can share?

We rented a tiny apartment that was within biking distance of our jobs. If you can live close to work, then you don't need a car. Our apartment was so small, that it didn't require much furniture, beyond a bed, a couch, and a table that doubled as a dining room table and a shared desk.

Each of us paid just $1 for our flip cell phones. They were nothing fancy, but they worked well enough. No cable TV subscription. Fortunately our apartment came with free high-speed Internet access.

We ate out about once a month. Every weekend we made giants pots of stew or casseroles that would last us the rest of the week. We always brewed our own coffee. No expensive Starbucks or Peet's lattes or cappuccinos.

We never needed an expensive gym membership, because our apartment came with its own workout room, and there was a nice lake across the street where we could jog or walk every day after work.

Most people overestimate what they need to be happy. We were newlyweds. We loved spending time with each other, and we enjoyed our jobs. We spent relaxing weekends at home together reading books, while our friends were spending $75 on cocktails every Friday and Saturday night. Neither my wife or I drink or smoke, so that saves some money too.

Did you ever go on vacation?

We always found a way to take one or two nice vacations every year. Some years we attended timeshare presentations at Disney World or Las Vegas in exchange for a free or reduced-price vacation. Other years, we just went bicycle touring.

Did you ever feel like you were missing out on the richer aspects of life?

Yes, and no. I would definitely have liked to have an iPhone over those years. Apart from that, there's not much to miss about a life of consumerism. It's pretty empty, and there's never an end in sight. No matter what gadget or service you buy, it's not going to fill the empty hole inside of yourself.

That hole can only be filled by meaningful relationships with family and friends.

What kind of stocks did you buy in your brokerage account?

We automatically invested 100% of our monthly savings into the SPY (the S&P 500 ETF) on the 20th day of every month. We had the brokerage do this automatically, so that we never had to login and see our profits or losses. We only bought the SPY, and never sold any, until recently when we cashed some out to buy a modest house and a car.

Do you have any kids?

Yes, one wonderful baby boy. My wife got pregnant shortly after we both retired. We recently bought an inexpensive house out in the country, where we can grow our own vegetables and raise chickens and maybe a few goats. Our overall cost of living has never been lower.

What are your plans for the future?

For now, we are going to just take it easy and focus on raising our child and spending time with each other. Once he goes off to kindergarten, we may go back to work. In the meantime, we would like to take a couple of trips and explore the world a bit. New Zealand, Bali, and the Great Barrier Reef are on our bucket list.

Thanks for taking the time to talk with me today.

7

OFF THE GRID MILLIONAIRE

Tell us a little bit about your early life.

I was born in the Bay Area. I never was much of a student, and spent most of my high school years working on cars in my parents' garage.

Did you attend college?

No, after high school, I went to work as a handyman for a property management company. It did not pay especially well, but the work was easy. Around this time, I started reading books and magazine articles about living off the grid. I remembered from high school about how Thoreau had lived in a small cabin in the woods, and figured that was something that I wanted to do too. I began to save up my money so that I could buy some land and get started.

Were you successful?

Yes, but it took me 15 years to save up the money. In 2001, real estate sales were really slow because of 9/11 and the bursting of the tech bubble. I found an amazing remote piece of property for sale-- 20 acres. It was tucked away in the hills south of San Jose. It also had a good producing well, and a small cabin that was just perfect. Lots of flat space to put a garden, barn, and other living structures if needed. They were asking $35,000, but I was able to get it for under $30,000 after a lot of negotiating.

When my apartment lease ended a few months later, I moved into the cabin and began to work on the property. I bought some chickens, and a goat, and planted a vegetable garden. Some of my friends have reminded me that I was also growing some pot, but I can neither confirm nor deny that.

It was great to be off the grid. I no longer had any utilities to pay. I started with a gasoline generator, but now have solar panels that supply all of my electricity. It was a little hot in the summer, but one nice thing about the Bay Area is the mild winters.

Were you able to quit your job?

That took me another 5 years. But I had a plan.

Now the Bay Area is such an expensive place to live because

of the housing. By buying this cheap cabin property, I had that taken care of.

I was growing a lot of my own food, and not paying anything for utilities. So I had those things taken care of too.

Now I needed to find a way to move to an all-cash lifestyle. I was tired of paying taxes and didn't like what the government was doing with my money, with all of the foreign wars and budget deficits.

Rents have always been sky-high in the South Bay, because of Silicon Valley. So I decided that I was going to create a cheap form of housing for people just getting started in tech who liked the idea of living off the grid.

I bought an old yellow school bus for $3,000 and parked it on the property. I gutted the inside and turned it into a pretty cool living space.

Whenever I had some cash, I bought some more housing for the property. I bought a yurt, a few used travel trailers, and few of those tiny houses.

Today it will cost you at least $2,000 for a studio apartment in San Jose. If you don't mind the commute and you love fresh air, you can choose instead to live on my property in the yellow school bus for $500 per month. That's a huge savings for someone who is trying to build up a down payment for a house. Some of the couples who live here have kids, and they really love living out in nature.

I quit my job about 3 years ago and can now live quite comfortably on the cash from my rentals. Everyone pays me cash, and I'm able to buy almost everything that I need using cash.

Do you have a bank account?

I do have a checking account, but I only use it for only one thing-- to pay off my credit card every month.

And I only use my credit card for 2 things: to pay Verizon for my iPhone, and to pay Amazon. I read a lot more books now than I ever did when I was younger.

I like living a mostly cash lifestyle. I don't have a mortgage, and I don't have to pay taxes. It's just me and my garden and my chickens. At night time, I can look up at the stars and breathe the fresh country air. Now I can't imagine living any other way. I would suffocate if I had to move back into the city.

I feel a little bad about not paying taxes, so recently I've begun to donate a lot of money to local homeless shelters. Sometimes I will bring a homeless person up here and let him live for free for a couple of months. They usually don't like it, though, because they want to be closer to their local drug dealer.

Aren't you afraid about getting caught by the IRS?

I used to be, but not anymore. I have a lot of money saved up, and would easily be able to pay the back taxes and penalties. And to hire a really good tax attorney.

Are you a millionaire then?

Yes, I am. And I'm actually making more money every year, since my rents keep rising and my expenses have stayed low. I suppose that Bay Area rents will level off one of these days, but they've kept rising quite quickly for the last few years.

Any final words of wisdom for the reader?

I'm not especially wise, but there are two quotes from Thoreau that have really guided me over the years:

"Go confidently in the direction of your dreams. Live the life you have imagined."

"All good things are wild and free."

Thanks for taking the time to talk with me today.

8

PET CREMATION PROFITS

Tell us a little bit about your early life.

    I was born in the same mid-sized Midwest city that I still live in today. I had a rather unremarkable childhood, spending most of my time cruising around on my bike and playing sports with my friends. I went to a state college, and married my high school sweetheart. I could afford to live anywhere these days, but I still enjoy the Midwest.

I like to watch the changing of the seasons. The snow is beautiful and great for snowmobiling. There are two fresh water lakes nearby that I enjoy fishing in. There's basically no crime to speak of. My roots go deep here. My body is made from the local dirt, and it will go back to the same dirt when I die. You couldn't pay me to live on the coasts and deal with the traffic, crime, and pollution.

What did you do after college?

I worked as a local real estate agent to save up money, but I really hated it. Nothing against the business, which has made many people rich, but it just wasn't for me. I really hated receiving phone calls at all hours, and having to take on the stress of my buyers and sellers.

While working as a real estate agent, I spent a lot of time researching other businesses. I tried to figure out which businesses would spit out the greatest amount of cash for the least amount of money invested. You write about capital-intensive businesses in some of your books-- those are the kind that I wanted to avoid. Charlie Munger talks about owning the types of businesses that just drown you in cash. That's what I wanted.

What was the conclusion of your research?

Surprisingly enough, I settled on pet cremation. It's one of the best businesses around. The margins are huge, and the startup costs are minimal. Basically all you need is a store-front and an oven. If you know anything about the wedding industry or the funeral industry, you know that the markups are huge. A $50 flower bouquet will cost you $150 for a wedding. A funeral home will buy an urn for $30, and then charge you $500. For some reason, capitalism doesn't work as well to bring down costs in emotional areas like weddings or funerals.

The same is true for pet cremation. I don't want to go into the details, but the markups are also quite large. A cremation oven is your biggest capital expenditure, but the natural gas to run it is still amazingly cheap.

So let's say that your family dog has just passed away. Now remember that this was the dog that your kids grew up with, and who sat on your lap when you became an empty nester. Fido was with you forever, and now he is dead.

You're not going to just put him out with the trash, which is disrespectful and probably also illegal. You could dig a big hole in your backyard, but that's a lot of work, and it's also probably against the HOA rules. Your wife loved that dog more than anything, and she wants him to have a proper and respectful end.

So you decide on cremation. Right now your deceased doggie is in the freezer at the vet. The dog weighs 80 pounds, so he's too heavy to transport on your own. You also don't like the idea of handling the corpse of man's best friend.

So you pay us to drive to the vet and transport the body to our crematorium. That's already a premium service that we charge for.

Now you have many choices to make, all of which make me a

lot of money. Do you want Fido cremated with a pile of other dogs, which is the more economic option? If you do, you'll end up with his ashes all mixed up with other dogs.

So you opt for a private cremation, which is another premium service. You could receive the ashes in a cardboard tube, but your wife wants something nicer. You could choose a beautiful Grecian urn. Or a hand-crafted glass keepsake. You could have the ashes put into an 18 carat gold locket that your wife can wear around her neck. These days you can even have your pet's ashes turned into a diamond. And there's another markup if you would like the diamond to be personally engraved.

You get the idea. On top of that, there are picture frames, photo albums, engraved plaques, etc. We make money on the cremation, but we also really make money on the upsells.

Do you ever feel guilty about charging a bereaved pet owner so much money?

I don't. No one has a gun to their head, and it's a completely optional service. All of our own family's pets were buried in our own backyard, and we're fine with that. It's legal to do that where we live. At the end of the day, you and me and our pets are just carbon anyway.

You can definitely tell that you're living in a wealthy society, when people can afford to lavish so much money on their pets, when they are alive and beyond. There is definitely a tailwind to the pet industry, with people having fewer children and choosing instead to lavish the same love, attention, and resources on pets.

Where do you invest your money?

I wish that I could reinvest it into my pet cremation business, but there is no need for the additional capital. My business already throws off more free cash than I know what to do with. I could start another pet cremation service in my city, but then I would probably be cannibalizing my own customers. As I said, I live in a medium-sized Midwest city, where there is only room for one main pet cremation business. My competitors are small and mostly incompetent. I'm the first listing on Google and Yelp for my area, so you can say that I have a local monopoly. I have a moat, as Warren Buffett would say.

In addition, I treat my customers well and with compassion. I know what it's like to lose a beloved pet, so I try to provide a bit of informal psychological counseling in my sales process. Whether I want it or not, it usually results in more upsells. That is the main way that families deal with grief in our culture.

So where do you invest your savings?

As I was saying, there's no room for another pet cremation business in my city. I could use my savings to start another one in a different city, but it would be a lot of work to manage. That's a head-ache that I don't need at my age. I already have more money than I know what to do with. I give generously to my church and local charities. The Federal and state governments always take more than they deserve. I don't like financing stupid wars in the Middle East or paying the interest on our huge national debt, but I pay my taxes anyway.

After taxes and charity, I only invest my money in Warren Buffett type companies. I've refined my process after reading your book Invest Like Warren Buffett. Today I own KO, WFC, AAPL, USB, AXP, KHC, MCO, LUV, MCD, and of course Berkshire Hathaway itself. I buy shares in these companies, and then never look at them again. My kids will inherit these holdings at a stepped-up cost basis, and so avoid paying any taxes on my capital gains.

What are the keys to being happy in life?

This is going to sound bad, but if you have a problem that money can solve-- and you have the money, then the problem just goes away. I've found that most problems can be solved with money. That's one of the strongest arguments that I know for making a lot of money.

Also, I live in a relatively low-cost Midwest town. The cost of living here is pretty low, and my wife and I don't have a lot of possessions. I've owned the big boat and the big RV, but then realized that big possessions end up owning you, rather than the other way around.

Any morning routines that you would like to share?

I like to eat a high-fat breakfast, with lots of coffee. If I eat something sweet for breakfast like pancakes, I tend to crash late morning. By sticking to bacon, sausage, and eggs, I find that my energy stays more even throughout the day. I like to rise with the sun, and then go to bed when the sun goes down. It's the same schedule that my chickens keep.

Can you recommend some of your favorite books that might be helpful to younger readers?

The Snowball Warren Buffett biography is really good. I also really enjoyed Walter Isaacson's biographies of Steve Jobs, Benjamin Franklin, and Leonardo Da Vinci. I tend to read only biographies these days. By reading them, I feel like I've lived multiple lives. Robert Greene's Mastery is also really good.

Anything else that you'd like to add?

Before you start your own business, think long and hard about the economics involved in the particular business model. How will it fare in an economic downturn? Will it make tons of money during boom times, and then lose tons of money during a recession? Is it the type of business that constantly requires new capital? Will you need to have your life savings tied up in inventory? How will you grow the business? Will it require lots of new capital to grow, or will you have to hire lots of new employees, with all of the headaches involved? Also, is it the type of business that is going to go away in the next 10 years? You definitely don't want to own something that goes the way of the buggy whip or typewriter.

Thanks for taking the time to talk with me today.

9

THE SKI BUM

W hat do you currently do for a living?

For the past 20 years, I've been a ski in-structor in Colorado during the winter. During the summer, I'm a whitewater rafting pilot. I've never made much money, but I pretty much get paid to do things that other people usually pay money to do.

How did you become a millionaire?

My grandfather passed away in the summer of 2006 and left me $30,000. At first I thought of getting a new car, but my old Tahoe was running fine, so I decided that I would invest the money instead. I didn't know much about the stock market at the time, but I had heard somewhere that you should invest in what you know.

So I opened up a brokerage account at Schwab and bought $10,000 worth of Blockbuster, $10,000 of Netflix (NFLX) and $10,000 of Vail Resorts (MTN).

Vail has always been my favorite ski area. When I wasn't skiing, I was watching movies from Blockbuster and Netflix (which used to operate a DVD mailing service).

Of course at the time, I wasn't smart enough to realize that Netflix would completely put Blockbuster out of business. I thought that somehow both companies could share the video rental market. It turns out that I was very very wrong.

So I had one stock that basically went to zero (Blockbuster). Then another stock (MTN) that went up 5x.

I made essentially all of my money in the third stock (NFLX), which has gone up 116x since I bought it.

How much is your brokerage account worth today (January 2019)?

About $1.25 million. It was worth a lot more just 12 months ago, but I try not to pay too much attention to that.

Will you ever sell your Vail or Netflix stock?

Maybe sometime in the future, but at this point, I'm still very bullish on both of them. Vail now runs multiple ski resorts across the country including Breckenridge and Vail in Colorado, and Northstar and Heavenly in California.

And Netflix has a lot of room to raise prices. I'd probably still pay 5x what I'm paying for my monthly subscription. I pay a lot more for my phone, and I get a lot less value from it.

I get a free Vail ski pass as an employee, but it seems that average folks still value it enough to pay upwards of $800 a year. Once you start with Vail or Netflix, you're probably a life-long customer.

Have you been smart or lucky in your investing?

Probably more lucky than smart. I would still recommend that people invest in what they know. That's always a better plan than relying on investment advice from other people. If you pick the stock yourself, then you'll have the courage to stick with it through thick and thin. That's harder to do with someone else's stock picks.

Thanks for taking the time to talk with me today.

10

THE QUANT TRADER

Tell us a little bit about your early life.

I grew up on the East Coast. I had a normal middle-class upbringing. When I was in the 3rd grade, it first occurred to me that I did not know how to be happy. I could see that my friends were happy and that many adults were happy. But it seemed a very foreign state to me. At this early age, I resigned myself to the fact that I would never be happy. In high school, I realized that maybe happiness wasn't everything. I realized that I could try to be successful, and that maybe that would compensate for my inability to be happy in life.

Things got much worse for me in college. So bad in fact that I made plans to commit suicide. I was just hours away from killing myself when I happened to receive a phone call from an old friend from middle school. I hadn't spoken with him in years. He was calling to thank me for having helped him many years previously. I couldn't even remember the incident, so it surprised me that it had made such a difference to him.

After the phone call, I looked down at my instruments of suicide in horror. I couldn't believe that I had come this close to actually killing myself. I immediately walked over to the mental health center on campus, and told them everything that had happened.

If my old friend had not called me when he did, I would not be alive today.

Since then, I've read many similar stories. Depression and other forms of mental illness are running rampant in America today.

So I would begin by saying to your readers, if you don't believe that you can be happy, you are wrong. There is just something wrong with your brain chemistry, and in most cases it can be fixed.

There's no shame in mental illness. It's not something that you chose, any more than someone chooses to be physically disabled.

Fortunately after many years of therapy and psychiatric drugs, I have now found that I can actually be happy.

Clinical depression can take on many forms. Many depressed people are high-functioning over-achievers. They fill their days with activities, so that they never have to confront the emptiness that they are feeling inside. Others experience depression as anxiety, low-energy, or the complete inability to get anything done.

If you think you might be depressed, talk to someone today, preferably a medical professional.

Untreated depression is very dangerous. It almost snuffed out my life right as it was beginning.

What did you study in college?

I double-majored in math and computer science. In my senior year, I began to get interested in the stock market. I never understood the old-fashioned gun-slinging type of traders who shot from the hip.

I guess I was a quant from my mother's womb. It occurred to me that the stock market, like any other phenomenon, could be modeled. It obviously required more complex and dynamic forms of modeling than some other realms, but it could nevertheless be modeled.

I began to explore academic papers on the subject. I studied momentum, mean-reversion, the small firm market anomaly, various seasonal and calendar effects, the value anomaly, market micro-structure anomalies, and many other subjects.

I was not impressed by the backtesting software that existed (this was in the mid 1990's), so I created my own. With the help of a couple professors, I was able to purchase market data to use in my backtesting.

At the end of the process, I had come up with a number of trading strategies that I thought would work well.

My math and CS professors were impressed as well. We pooled their money with friends and family money, and I was able to launch my first hedge fund— just months before graduating from college.

In retrospect, I was very lucky. I've never had to get a real job. Over the years, the fund has grown to just under $30 million. The trading strategies have changed over the years, as the market has changed, but my underlying quantitative and empirical approach has remained the same. I've chosen to keep the fund relatively small, so that I can pursue trading strategies that will not work with larger amounts of capital.

Can you give us an example of a trading strategy that you currently use in the fund?

The momentum anomaly has been quite strong over the past 5 years, as you discuss in your books. Whether this continues remains to be seen. There are complex quantitative ways to measure if a trading strategy has stopped working. Looking at maximum historical drawdowns compared to a present drawdown is one simple way to approach it. It remains to be seen if the momentum anomaly works as well over the next 5 years as it worked over the past 5 years.

Can you give us an example of a powerful trading strategy that stopped working?

Yes, back in 2008 and 2009, it was very profitable to maintain a market-neutral positioning that involved shorting both the FAZ (Direxion Daily Financial Bear 3X ETF) and the FAS (Direxion Daily Financial Bull 3X ETF) in equal dollar amounts. If one side got too overweight, you would rebalance, so that you were market-neutral. Leveraged ETFs are notorious for going to zero over time, especially in volatile markets. So I thought, why not profit from this tendency, all the while maintaining a market-neutral portfolio.

Unfortunately in 2009 and 2010, there was a lot of coverage of this strategy in the financial blogosphere, and it stopped working. It may have also stopped working simply because market volatility fell off a cliff and never recovered (until fairly recently). There's a decent chance that this strategy could start working again if market volatility stays high over the next couple of years. Only time will tell.

It's important as a quant trader to be constantly evolving. Trading strategies appear, and then suddenly stop working, so you need to be constantly researching new approaches. I don't think that I can compete with the big quants like Renaissance Technologies, which is the main reason that I've chosen to keep my assets under management relatively small.

What do your annual returns look like?

My fund has returned more than 25% annualized over the last 20 years.

What do you like to do in your free time?

As strange as it may sound, I like to design and build toy airplanes, kites, and drones. I guess I'm still a kid at heart.

Any advice for our younger readers?

Learn to check in with yourself to see how you are feeling every day. Life is so short. There's no time to be unhappy. Maybe you aren't eating right or getting enough sleep, or maybe you have some underlying psychiatric conditions that should be investigated. Either way, don't compromise.

Any morning routines or life hacks that you would like to share?

I swear by cryotherapy, cold plunges, and icy showers. Not only do they boost the immune system, but they also provide instant pain relief and elevation of mood. If you live by a cold body of water, try jumping into it every day before breakfast. It's difficult at first, but becomes much easier over time. Start by immersing just your legs, then move on to the rest of your body. Start with 30 seconds, then gradually increase the time as you build tolerance.

I also use oily fish (like sardines), dark chocolate, and oysters to brighten my mood when I am feeling down. I can't explain the physiology, but I do know that they work well for me.

Where do you invest your own money?

I have 95% of my net worth invested in my own hedge fund. I believe that you shouldn't be a chef if you're not willing to eat your own cooking.

Thanks for taking the time to talk with me today.

11

THE CANNABIS CAPITALIST

Tell us a little bit about your early life.

I was born and grew up on the East coast, in a mid-sized town. I think I've always been an entrepreneur at heart. In elementary school, I used to buy bags of Starburst candy for $2.00 and then sell the individual pieces to my friends for 10 cents apiece. I seem to remember that there were about 70 pieces in a bag, so I was netting $5.00. It was easy money. I was also one of those kids who actually had a lemonade stand. My brother and I had so much fun running that thing every summer.

What did you study in college?

Ostensibly, anthropology. It was a complete joke of a major, but at least it was easy. I spent most of my time gambling online and offline. Lots of blackjack and poker. I'm probably still in the casino database for card-counters.

Did you start any businesses in college?

Not really. I was experimenting with SEO-optimized websites that were monetized using Google AdSense, but they never made any serious money. I was making much more money with my gambling. My parents weren't happy, but at least I was leading the life that I wanted.

What did you do after college?

Much to the relief of my parents, who thought I was going to become a professional gambler, I got a real job. I went to work for a Bay Area tech company on the non-technical side of things. It was a great place to work, and the perks were amazing. Free food, company gyms, in-house massage therapists, amazing speaker programs. Everything was great except for the fact that I was still an employee, and there was a lot of stress. People in the Bay Area never brag about how much money they are making, but rather about the long hours that they are working. Being busy is the new status symbol.

I hated that, as well as the traffic and high cost of living. I was making a lot of money, but most of it was going to taxes and housing.

At the same time, I began to develop lots of health conditions: neck and lower back pain, asthma, and chronic sinus infections. I was then diagnosed with degenerative disc disease, which helped to explain why my lower back pain had become so bad. It became increasingly difficult for me to sit at a desk, or even stand at a standing desk. My doctor began to prescribe stronger and stronger pain-killers, which worked but definitely affected my mental state. I have real compassion for opiate addicts in our country, and might have ended up in a similar situation if it were not for a discovery.

What was that?

CBD oil. It's one of the major components of marijuana, but it does not have a psychoactive effect. It does not and cannot get you high. It's the THC in marijuana that gets you high, and there is usually no THC in CBD oil.

As soon as I started taking just a small dose of CBD, my back pain went away. Surprisingly, my sinus infections and asthma symptoms also went away. I stopped taking pain-killers and inhalers. My mood improved markedly.

Now even though I had smoked some pot in college, I always considered medical marijuana to be a bit of a joke. I thought it was just an another excuse to get high and a sneaky stepping-stone on the path to full legalization. I used to think: "Of course if you get high, you are not going to notice your medical maladies as much. You could also treat them with whiskey."

What I never realized, until I did the research, was that cannabis is a natural anti-inflammatory. It doesn't just mask things, but it also heals them. It is the single best medicine that we have to treat chronic pain, migraines, nausea, epilepsy, and even cancer, multiple sclerosis, and Parkinson's. That's the reason that I prefer the scientific name "cannabis" over "marijuana." The latter carries too much baggage in the popular imagination.

You sound like quite the evangelist.

That's one of the problems with talking about cannabis. It is actually such a powerful medicine that you can't help but sound a little crazy when you talk about all of its benefits. But this should not be too surprising to us. Cannabis has been used in traditional Chinese and Indian medicine for thousands of years. The ancient Greeks also used cannabis as medicine. This is not some drug that was just synthesized yesterday. Once you try cannabis, and CBD in particular, you realize why the makers of over-the-counter analgesics and prescription opiates might not want this stuff legalized. CBD completely stopped my back pain, and did not make me feel woozy and stupid like opiates did. It is also completely safe for the liver, unlike ibuprofen and acetaminophen, where it's pretty easy to take a toxic dose.

Doesn't cannabis make you stoned and stupid?

That's one of the biggest misconceptions out there. You

would actually be surprised to learn how many coders in Silicon Valley use cannabis on the job when they are writing code. These are high IQ, super-productive people. They are definitely not stoners or losers.

There are certain kinds of cannabis that will make you stupid and unable to get off of the couch. Smoke a strain that is high in myrcene and THC and you will not be getting anything productive done for the rest of the day. Indicas have this reputation.

But there are also strains of cannabis that will give you energy and mental clarity and focus that are even better than a strong cup of coffee. Try one of the sativas like Lemon Haze or Green Crack. The names are funny, but we are talking about some serious medicine here.

There are literally over a hundred active "cannabinoids" in the cannabis plant. And their action is modulated by the particular concentration of each in a particular strain of cannabis. Then there are also the "terpenes" (or aromatic compounds) that modulate the behavior of these cannabinoids. Some terpenes will give you mental clarity, some will knock you out on the couch. Once you understand the chemistry involved, you can pick the strain of cannabis that you need at the moment. Whether you're looking for a burst of energy, or help getting to sleep, there's a strain of cannabis for you.

All of which is to say that cannabis is medicine. I think Bob Marley was right on this. It's a shame that the 1960's and stoners from all decades have given cannabis a bad name.

So you think it should be legal?

Yes, definitely. It needs to be legalized, and even more, it needs to be studied by the scientific community. We are still in the first inning of studying cannabis as medicine. And it's going to be hard to make this happen until it is removed from being a Schedule 1 drug in the U.S. It's absurd. A Schedule 1 drug is defined to be any drug that has a high potential for abuse and zero medical usage. In fact, cannabis has more medical uses than any other plant in the world. I believe that we live in a mad world, where oxycontin is legal, but cannabis is not.

But you don't have to take my word for it. If you have lower back pain or any pain at all, just give CBD oil a try.

This is fascinating stuff, but let's return to the topic of money. Before our digression, your health was getting better thanks to CBD, but you were still an employee at a big tech company.

Yes, I was still working at the same company. But as my health began to improve and my energy levels rose, I couldn't stop telling people about how well the CBD oil had worked. My co-workers and girlfriend got tired of all my proselytizing. But I couldn't stop talking about it, particularly as I continued to research medical cannabis. So I started a blog to share with the world what I was learning in real time. Then I expanded it to a YouTube channel, Twitter, Facebook, etc.

At this point, I was spending all of my free time making new videos and writing blog posts about my cannabis discoveries. It never felt like work for a moment. In fact, I would hurry home from my official job, and then work on my cannabis blog well into the early morning hours. The feedback from my readers was enormously gratifying. I was hearing from people from every walk of life whose health conditions were being healed by CBD and cannabis. I was hearing from sick people who were getting well, as well as from healthy people who were figuring out new ways to use cannabis to increase stamina, productivity, cognitive functioning, and creativity.

It was about this time that I started listening to Pat Flynn's podcast and reading his Smart Passive Income blog. It was here that I first learned about how to do affiliate marketing. Affiliate marketing is where you sell someone's product, and then get a percentage of the revenues. Most people have heard of Amazon's affiliate program. But it turns out that there were also affiliate programs being run by companies that sold CBD oil, cannabis tinctures, terpenes, seeds, pipes, online courses on how to grow cannabis, etc.

As I began to tell my readers about these products (all of

which I was using myself, so I knew that they were good), I began to receive affiliate commissions. First it was just a few hundred dollars a month. Then a few thousand. Then $10,000 per month and up from there. As my YouTube channel became more popular, I was also able to monetize it.

As soon as I hit $15,000 per month, I quit my job. I've never looked back. To this day, I still can't believe that I get paid to research and talk about one of my passions. Strangers still roll their eyes when they learn about what I do for a living. My hope is that as more states legalize cannabis for medical and recreational use, the stigma surrounding cannabis will disappear. I'm certainly not a stoner or loser. I'm married, have 2 kids, pay my taxes, and drive within the speed limit (and certainly never after partaking of cannabis).

So I take it that it was this affiliate income that made you a millionaire?

Yes.

Where do you invest your money?

After reading your book on Warren Buffett, I've begun to buy some Buffett stocks. But I'm afraid that most of my net worth is currently sitting in a few high-yield savings accounts. I'm too busy to spend time investing it actively.

Any advice for high school or college students?

This is going to sound funny coming from me, but I would

advise them to completely stay away from all alcohol and drugs, including cannabis. Wait until your body is done growing before you partake of any of these. When you're young, you don't need any sort of drugs or supplements to get by. You have youth, and there's nothing better. When you get older and start to experience the aches and pains of middle age, then look into cannabis.

What are the keys to being happy in life?

Good friendships, and a good spouse. Money doesn't change anything. If you're a jerk, you'll still be a jerk when you're rich. If you are in bad health, you'll still be in bad health, until you learn how to take care of yourself. The best thing about having some money in the bank is the freedom to create your own daily schedule. If you are feeling productive, you can stay up working all night, and not have to worry about making it into the office the next day. If you are tired and unproductive, you don't have to sit at your desk and pretend to be busy.

Any morning routines that you would like to share?

I don't eat anything until about 1 pm or 2 pm. I have a cup of coffee (or sometimes some Jack Herer or Super Lemon Haze cannabis) when I first wake up at 6 am, but usually nothing else. When I am engrossed in my work, I find that I'm naturally not hungry until the early afternoon. Once I start eating, I find that I'm less productive.

Can you recommend a favorite book that might be helpful to younger readers?

All of your trading books are great. They're short, easy-to-read, and full of actionable tips.

If you're looking for fiction, you can't go wrong with Proust, Dostoevsky, or any of the novels of W. Somerset Maugham. The Moon and Sixpence is fantastic as a loosely fictionalized version of the life of the painter Paul Gauguin.

Any parting thoughts?

Live each day as if it's going to be your last day on earth. Take time to watch the sunset and hug your loved ones.

Thanks for taking the time to talk with me today.

12

THE MOMENTUM TRADER

Tell us a little bit about your early life.

The central memory of my childhood is a tragic one. When I was in the 3rd grade and my older brother was in the 5th grade, he was struck and killed by a drunk driver as we were walking home from school one afternoon. He was the really talented kid in our family, and I often wonder what he would have gone on to achieve if he had lived.

Ever since that defining event, I've always been a pretty serious person. I think that when my brother died, it was the beginning of my adult view of the world, even though I was only 8 years old. I've had this sense about how short and fragile our lives are. This belief, rather than paralyzing me, gives me energy and helps me every day to try to focus on the really important things.

The ancients called this *memento mori*, the practice of the remembrance of death. Steve Jobs understood this well, and it is probably one reason why he accomplished so much. His 2005 Stanford University commencement address is really worth listening to a few times a year to be reminded of the power of *memento mori*.

I still ask myself every day why my brother died and I lived. As I've said, he was definitely the more talented one. I guess some amount of survivor's guilt is inevitable. I've tried to transmute this grief and guilt into a form of energy that propels me forward in life. I try to make every day count. If that car had been a few inches further onto the sidewalk, I would have been dead as well. So my whole life has been an unearned gift.

Life itself is so beautiful. It is a beautiful gift from the universe, as are all of the wonderful people that I meet every day. I think my experience has helped to make me a kinder person. I always try to give people the benefit of the doubt. A lot of the rude or angry people that you meet are carrying very heavy hidden burdens in their hearts.

What was your introduction to trading and the markets?

In 1998, I was still working a safe and boring white-collar job, when I came across the original Market Wizards book in a local used book store. I still remember that evening when I first cracked open the book and then stayed up all night finishing it.

I could not believe my eyes. Here were people who were actually making enormous sums of money by simply calling in orders over the phone (the originals interviews were made before the Internet). At the time, I was making about $60,000 a year, and spending most of it as quickly as I made it.

After reading Market Wizards, I decided that I was going to start setting aside money every month, so that I could open up my own trading account. I figured that I could cut my expenses enough to put aside $10,000 every year for 5 years, until I had $50,000 which seemed like a decent amount to start trading with.

As it turned out, I had been too optimistic and was only able to save about $5,000 per year. So it took me almost a decade to save up that $50,000.

Picture this: I've just opened up my first brokerage account with the $50,000 and I'm all ready to start trading when. . . Lehman Brothers collapses (this was September 2008), and the whole world is plunged into the financial crisis. I was too scared to place a trade, partially because stock prices were moving so quickly, and the amount of bad news coming out every day was hard to digest. It had taken me 10 years to save up that money, so I wasn't about to blow it in a stupid way.

After a few months of paralysis, I began to build up my courage again. I remember hearing President Obama saying in early March 2009 that he thought it was a good time to invest. As it turned out, he called (or caused?) the exact bottom of the bear market. Obama's words gave me the encouragement that I needed to place my first trade.

So in early March 2009, I began to buy all of the stocks that I knew really well, because I used their products: Amazon, Apple, Netflix, Select Comfort (now known as Sleep Number), and Whole Foods. Within a week or so, I was fully invested in these stocks. I was so bullish on these companies, and I figured that I was doing exactly what the professionals say you should do: "Buy stocks when there is blood in the streets."

I got really lucky with my timing. I paid something like 40 cents for my Sleep Number shares, and just 12 months later, it was trading above 10. All of the other stocks that I had picked did really well too. So in April 2010, I sold off all of my positions and went to cash. I never expected the rally to last another 8 years, as it has. I had made a lot of money since the March 2009 bottom, and I was scared to give back any of it. The more that I read, the more that I realized that I needed to trade my own strategies, rather than just depending on a bull market to make me money.

What stock trading strategies did you use then?

In my reading of technical papers, I kept coming across references to the "momentum anomaly" and PEAD or "post-earnings announcement drift." I've made most of my money since 2010 trading PEAD, particularly in tech stocks. The basic market anomaly is this: when a stock reports an earnings surprise and gaps up or down sharply, it has a strong tendency to continue to moving in the same direction for a few days, or even a few weeks.

How do we know when an earnings surprise has taken place? You don't want to look at the actual earnings number, but rather at the market's reaction. I know that you are always preaching the same thing in your books: "Don't trade the news, but rather the market's reaction to the news."

A big gap in either direction after an earnings report is your proof that the market has been surprised. A stock will usually continue moving in that same direction, as big institutional investors are forced to adjust their positions. As a little guy, you can ride this wave. I've done especially well trading this with call options. After earnings are out, implied volatility immediately collapses, which makes call options cheaper. You definitely don't want to buy these call options before earnings, or you will have to pay up, due to elevated implied volatility. So I usually buy an at-the-money or slightly out-of-the-money call option on the morning after earnings, in order to play this post-earnings announcement drift. That has worked quite well the past few years. It's been my bread and butter trade.

We've recently had a great example of PEAD with Apple hitting a trillion dollar market cap after reporting earnings this summer. Take a look at a chart of AAPL: after the market closed on 31 July 2018, Apple reported earnings. The next day, it gapped up on the earnings surprise and continued to rise for almost a month.

Can you tell us about some other trading strategies that have been working lately?

Yes, one of my favorites is what I call the "Death Star" trade. There's this popular misconception that Amazon or Facebook or Google are able to completely and instantly destroy the competition once they enter a new vertical. Sort of like the Death Star sailing in and blowing up the planet Alderaan. So for example, in September 2016, Amazon announced that it would be getting into photo-printing business. If you're a parent, you've probably made those Shutterfly photo books of your kids. When Amazon made this announcement, Shutterfly's stock (SFLY) sold off quite sharply, and continued to go down for a few weeks.

Now it is true that Amazon actually can wipe out its competition over the long run. We saw that happen with brick-and-mortar book stores. But the stock market has a tendency to over-react to this sort of announcement in the short run.

The basic Death Star strategy involves buying one of these smaller tech stocks like Shutterfly once it's been beaten up by an announcement from Amazon, Facebook, or Google. You don't want to buy the stock on the same day of the announcement, but rather wait a few weeks for the bad news to get completely priced in. It usually turns out that the big Death Star company has better things to do than destroy its competition in a small niche. By November 2016, SFLY had completely recovered from its sell-off, and I made some very nice money playing this recovery.

The same thing happened just this year to MTCH (parent company of Tinder, Match.com, and OkCupid), when Facebook announced that they were going to launch a dating feature. User engagement among younger people has been sharply declining on Facebook, and presumably Facebook wanted to give them a good reason to spend more time on its platform. As is usually the case, MTCH crashed on the announcement, but then recovered again this summer, going on to hit new all-time highs.

Again, this is a short to medium-term trade. You are playing a temporary over-reaction in the market. Over the long term, these large tech Death Stars can certainly inflict a lot of damage on the competition.

You started your trading account with $50,000. How much money are you trading these days?

I now have just over $1.2 million in my trading account, even after paying a lot of money in taxes. I was able to quit my job a few years ago, and I've never looked back.

Any other trading strategies that you'd like to share?

I've been using your Rocket Stocks strategy ever since I first read about it in 2016. I was trading a version of rocket stocks with my PEAD strategy before that, but your book helped me to generalize the strategy and not to be so afraid of stocks that were trading at 52-week, or even all-time highs. Trading call options on rocket stocks has worked really well for me.

Any morning routines or life hacks that you would like to share?

The best part of my morning routine is always the coffee. This is one of those secrets that is hidden in plain view. If you don't already drink coffee, you really should consider it. I never drank coffee until I turned 30 years old. Before that, I mostly drank tea or water. But then I kept reading interviews with famous people who attributed their success and creativity to coffee.

Once I started drinking coffee, I can honestly tell you that my productivity doubled or tripled. I'm not exaggerating here. You don't want to overdo it, but one or two cups of coffee (maybe with cream, but little to no sugar) is almost guaranteed to sharpen your mind and make you more productive than you already are. I'll leave figuring out the reasons to the biochemists in the audience. I am just a pragmatist, and try to do what works.

There is one additional life hack that I would like to mention. When I was in my 20's, I was obsessed with Napoleon. I still think that he is one of those people who really repays studying. One of his routines involved reading and rereading about the military campaigns of Alexander the Great, Caesar and other great military leaders. When I first learned this, I tried to extrapolate it to my own life.

My answer was to create my own "swipe file" that I review on a regular basis. I like this to be an actual file of physical papers, so it feels real and tangible.

What do you include in this swipe file?

I include anything that has really made a big impression on me. Sometimes you read an article in a magazine or online, and you find that it really inspires you and gives you energy whenever you reread it. So I try to save anything like that that really stands out. This file also includes my typewritten notes on all of the trading books that I have ever read. Reading and rereading these trading notes really helps me to stay focused on what matters most in the markets. I can tell you that I have included your entire book <u>The Little Black Book of Stock Market Secrets</u> in my file. It's like a mini swipe file on its own.

My swipe file also includes my notes on diet and nutrition,

hacks and habits to optimize sleep and waking energy, as well as reminders about how best to relate to other people and have charisma.

Most often, we don't need to learn new things, but rather we need to be reminded of what we already know.

I read through this file at the beginning of every month, or whenever I'm feeling tired, lost, or low energy. Often I will just skim through the file, and whatever I need most at that moment will jump out at me.

You should create your own swipe file in a way that works for you. It might include YouTube videos, or even movies, that inspire you and give you energy. Then set a reminder on your calendar to review this file regularly.

If you do this, you'll be ahead of 99% of people. Most people don't make a conscious effort to remember the important lessons that they have learned.

Thanks for taking the time to talk with me today.

13

THE 6-YEAR MILLIONAIRE

Tell us a little bit about your early life.

I was born in Florida, but my parents moved to Nevada when I was five years old. My parents never gambled much. Neither do I, except in the stock market, as we shall see. I only like to play when there are really good odds. I was an average student in high school, but pretty good at math. I ended up studying accounting at the local university and then got a job in the Las Vegas area.

Where were you 6 years ago?

In 2013, I was in a white-collar office job making just over $60,000 per year. It was boring, but pretty easy work.

The most important turning point in my life happened when I casually picked up a copy of Tim Ferriss' book The 4-Hour

Work Week. I stayed up all night reading it. I loved his idea of starting a business on the side as a way of creating more financial and lifestyle freedom. At first I didn't have a good idea of how to start. Then I came across the "Shopify Build a Business Contest" that Richard Branson and Tim Ferriss were promoting. The basic idea was that you open up an online store on Shopify. The new stores that generated the highest sales over a certain period of time would win a trip to Richard Branson's private island, or something like that. I didn't end up winning the contest but it still changed my life.

What did your online store sell?

I sold antique collectibles and other cool stuff that I found at local garage sales. Things like old Polaroid cameras, vintage clothing and jewelry, old posters and records, and other antiques that you might have found in your grandparents' basement. My profit margins were enormous because I basically bought stuff that no one wanted, and then cleaned it or fixed it up. Never underestimate the power of nostalgia to sell goods. And never underestimate how high your profit margins can be when you have a very low cost of goods sold (COGS).

In the meantime, I was really impressed by how easy Shopify made it for me to set up my online store. They had basically cracked the e-commerce code in a way that Yahoo stores and other competitors had failed to do. I told everyone at work about Shopify, but people in accounting departments are not too interested in this kind of thing. My vintage store continued to grow and grow. I needed capital to grow my inventory, so I decided to do something that seemed pretty crazy at the time. I moved out of the house that I was renting and into a small room in someone's house. I sold my car, cancelled my cell phone and cable, and stopped eating out. By making these changes, I was able to save over 70% of my post-tax income. It wasn't very fun downsizing like that, but it gave me the capital that I needed to increase my inventory and online sales. My store continued to grow for the next few years, and I was able to reinvest both my profits and most of my salary into that growth. Eventually I had to rent a storage locker to hold my inventory.

Fast forward a few years to when I heard that Shopify was going public. This was May 2015. Immediately after the IPO, I began using all of my excess cash to buy Shopify stock. As I liquidated my online store inventory, I used the cash to buy more Shopify stock. I also used every last penny from my salary that I could spare to buy even more stock.

I think it was Andrew Carnegie who said that the best way to become rich is to "put all of your eggs in one basket and then watch that basket." Of course you have to be very careful about picking the basket, but I think that advice is right. You are never going to become rich quickly by investing in a diversified portfolio of blue-chip dividend companies. It can work, but it just takes too long. I did not want to wait until I was 70 years old to be wealthy.

How did you know that Shopify stock was the right basket into which to put all of your eggs?

My accounting background definitely helped. Shopify's revenue growth was amazing, and I was very familiar with the product. In early 2018, I realized that if Shopify's stock was going where I thought it was going, I would make more money if I liquidated my Shopify store and used the proceeds to buy more Shopify stock and options.

2019 has been an amazing year for me. I was able to identify the monthly breakout in Shopify in February 2019, and then really leverage that breakout to my advantage using risk reversals and out-of-the-money call options. Your books and videos on momentum stocks really helped me to analyze the situation and take full advantage of it.

Do you still have a full position in Shopify?

No, I exited most of my position in July 2019. I still have a 10% position, but I'm really worried about bad financial news on the horizon. I don't have a good sense of how bad the flat yield curve and China trade war are, but I know that I never want to go back to being poor.

What are you currently invested in?

I still have 10% of my net worth in SHOP. I have 20% in

Bitcoin, and another 10% in the gold ETF (GLD). Another 30% will be in a personal residence and maybe an investment rental. I hope to be able to buy a large property with a guest house at the other end of the property that I can rent out to help to pay my bills. I'll hold the remainder of my net worth in high-yield savings accounts and CD's. I certainly won't miss living in a room in someone else's house.

Do you mind sharing your net worth?

After I pay all of my 2019 taxes, I should end up with just over $1.8 million. Fortunately I live in a state that does not have a state income tax.

Have you quit your job yet?

No, but I plan to quit before the end of the year, and then take some time off to focus on Bitcoin and other crypto developments.

Thanks for taking the time to talk with me today.

14

THE HUSTLER

Tell us a little bit about your early life.

I was born in San Francisco. We moved to Fresno when I was five, because my father's business failed. Unfortunately, my father never recovered from that failure. Some people are able to bounce back from that sort of thing, but not him. In Fresno, he just bounced around from odd job to odd job. He had a drinking problem, and so was never able to stay in the same place for long. We moved from apartment to apartment, and were lucky when we could pay the rent on time.

I love my father, but I promised myself from a very early age that I would never be like him. I don't drink or do any drugs. That gives me a real advantage when dealing with the general population who these days is usually drunk or high.

What did you do after high school?

I just had to get out of Fresno, so I moved to Pasadena. The climate is so much nicer there. I worked first as a dishwasher, then as a waiter. I didn't have the time or money for college. I hadn't learned anything useful in high school, and college looked like a high-priced version of the same thing.

In Pasadena, I used to drive through the rich neighborhoods, looking at the giant fenced lots and amazing houses. I wondered how some people were able to have so much, while I had so little. I spent all of my free time at the local library and on the internet researching how to get rich.

What did you discover?

Robert Kiyosaki's book "Rich Dad Poor Dad" had a big influence on me. His description of "Poor Dad" sounded just like my father, living from paycheck to paycheck, and always just scraping by. After reading this book, I realized that there was a better way to live than selling your time for money. I really liked the idea of passive income, and wanted to figure out how to set it up in my own life.

At the time, I was living in a fancier apartment than I needed. When my lease was up, I decided to downsize to a room in someone's house. It was not a happy day, but I realized what I needed to do. At the time, I had no savings, and I always spent everything that I earned on rent, eating out, and stupid things that I didn't really need. By downsizing to a single room, I was able to finally start saving money every month. I also stopped eating out completely. I would make these giant pots of vegetable stew and rice, and eat it for every meal. I started shopping for clothes at Goodwill and thrift shops.

Finally the money started to pile up in my savings account. In fact, I was saving about 50% of my paycheck every month. But it still wasn't enough-- at this rate, I would never get rich.

It was around this time that I discovered Fiverr.com. I was looking for ways to make some extra money online in my free time when I came across this website. Fiverr basically lets you perform online services for $5 or more (hence the name). I've always had a good singing voice. So I submitted a listing where people would pay me $5 to sing happy birthday to a loved one (I would record the song and deliver it as a digital file). By adding some upgrades like rush delivery or personalizing the song more, I was able to charge closer to $10-$15 per song. Pretty soon, I was making an extra $150/day just recording songs on Fiverr.

That seems like a fun way to make an extra $50,000 per year. So you were basically working as a waiter and singing?

That's not all. It was about this time that Uber came to LA. It's not as profitable now, but in those early days, you could make some really good money by driving. So in addition to waiting tables and singing for Fiverr, I was also driving for Uber.

That's crazy.

Yes, I was only sleeping about 4-5 hours per day at the time. All of my waking hours were spent driving for Uber, working as a waiter, and singing songs for Fiverr.

You must have been exhausted, juggling all of those things.

Yes, and no. I was definitely tired all of the time. But I had more energy than I had ever had before. It's hard to explain. I think that when you know that you are on the path to something better, having that purpose gives you a secret source of energy. I knew I was on the path to getting rich. My life finally had a purpose and a plan.

So what was the plan exactly?

The plan was to make as much money as possible, spend as little as possible, and invest the difference in the stock market. I knew Mexicans who regularly sent more than half of their earnings back to their family in Mexico. Rather than paying my family (I was single at the time), I decided to "pay myself first" just like in <u>Rich Dad Poor Dad</u>.

Did you end up buying some stocks?

Yes. I used to watch Jim Cramer on CNBC. His investing philosophy made a lot of sense to me: you want to own the stocks that represent the future, and that control their markets. So I began to buy his FANG stocks with whatever cash I had on hand: Facebook, Amazon, Netflix, and Google. I was also buying Apple at the time, so I felt pretty proud when it was added to create the FAANG.

Do you still own these stocks?

Yes, I've never sold a share.

Are you still renting a room in someone's house?

No. I got married in early 2017, and my wife and I have our own place now. She's a great cook, so I don't need to eat stew every day anymore.

Are you a millionaire now?

Yes, I have just over $1 million in my brokerage account, all in FAANG stocks.

Do you think you'll ever sell them?

Probably not. These are big global companies. I think they are unstoppable.

Do you still wait tables or drive an Uber?

No. My wife and I started a property management company right before we got married. It's great to be in business together. And, no, I don't miss being a waiter at all.

Property management is a great business to be in, since it

doesn't require any significant cash or loans to start. There's no inventory, no expensive equipment required, so it doesn't tie up a lot of capital. I wanted to start a business that wouldn't require me to sell any of my FAANG shares. We even run it out of a home office. We get to keep 7-10% of the monthly rent on a growing portfolio of single family homes, in exchange for dealing with tenants, repair, etc.

Our income should continue to grow over time, and I'm confident I won't have to touch my FAANG shares until retirement. Property management is not exactly the passive income that I once dreamed of, but my wife and I hope to be able to funnel a significant part of our earnings into rental properties, Treasuries, and muni bonds. If I ever decided to sell my FAANG shares and move the money into munis, they would generate significant annual cash flow that was tax-free at the Federal and state levels.

Any parting thoughts?

If I could do this, anyone can do it. Make some big sacrifices over the next 3-5 years. Live way below your means, and start to invest-- whether it is in stocks or real estate or just CD's. You definitely have to learn to hustle if you are going to get rich, but it's worth it. In just a short time, you can really change your life.

Thanks for taking the time to talk with me today.

15

THE MILLIONAIRE MUSICIAN

Where do you live, and what do you do for a living?

I've always lived in the Deep South. I live in the same house that my grandaddy built and that my daddy grew up in. My day job is being a real estate agent. At night, I'm also a professional musician.

What instruments do you play?

I play guitar and mandolin-- mostly bluegrass music. It's a style of music that comes out of the string band music of the American South. Bill Monroe added high tenor singing, a rhythmic driving mandolin sound, as well as the rolling banjo of Earl Scruggs. The result was a hard-driving original American folk sound. It's now played not only all around the country, but all around the world. For example, some of the best bluegrass musicians that I've ever known live in Japan.

Does being a bluegrass musician pay well?

I can answer that one with a joke:

Question: What's the difference between a banjo player and a large pepperoni pizza?

Answer: A large pepperoni pizza can feed a family of four.

Lots of musicians complain that the profession doesn't pay well enough. But the way I look at it, you're getting paid to do something that many people will gladly do for free in their spare time. If something is really fun, it shouldn't pay that well. I can understand why lawyers and tax accountants get paid well, since very few people would want to do that kind of work for free.

So your major source of income must be from your work as a real estate agent?

Yes. I'm paid on commission.

I don't know how it works in other parts of the country, but I can tell you how it works here. The seller of a house normally pays the commission. The selling agent will usually charge him 5-6% of the selling price. Let's say 6% to make the math easy here. The selling agent gets to keep 3%

and the buyer's agent gets to keep 3%. In addition, each agent must pay his broker half of that, or 1.5%.

So if I help someone sell their house, I usually get to keep 1.5% of the selling price. If I help a buyer purchase a house, I usually get 1.5% of the purchase price. Now obviously everything is negotiable in real estate, but that's how the general numbers work.

In my town, most houses cost between $100,000 and $300,000, so I am making about $1,500 to $4,500 per house. Now quite often, I will be representing both the buyer and the seller. In those cases, I will make double those amounts, or $3,000 to $9,000 per house.

I have a real advantage, because I've lived here my whole life, and I know everyone. My wife is from this same town too. When it comes time to buy a house or sell a house, almost everyone uses me. They know that I'm honest and that I'll get the job done the right way.

So you have a sort of local monopoly?

Yes, I guess that's what you could call it. At this point, I'm able to give back a lot to the community. I've paid for other people's kids to go off to college, and I give a lot back to my church and local community. If you're going through a rough time, I won't even charge you to sell your house.

Are you a millionaire?

Yes, I am, but you won't believe how it happened. I've been playing guitar and mandolin since I was a kid. I've always had the collector's bug, not because I like to collect, but because I like having some nice instruments around to play.

For the last 40 years, whenever I've had some extra cash, it's gone into instruments. It drives my wife crazy, but it's made us millionaires. That was never the plan, but the Lord has blessed us through these instruments.

I own a number of pre-war Martin guitars. Most of them were made during the Great Depression by master craftsmen. You see, Martin had to fire everyone except the best craftsmen, because it was a depression. These guitars are made with Brazilian rosewood and Adirondack spruce that you just can't find today. Brazilian rosewood is an endangered rain forest tree these days.

I also own a few Loar mandolins that are worth more than $150,000 each. I paid nothing close to that for them. I think they've gone up more than the stock market itself since I bought them.

Together, all of my guitars and mandolins are easily worth more than $1 million. Maybe even $1.5 million.

Have you ever sold any of your vintage instruments?

Not so far. My wife and I are in our late 60's now, so you never know what's coming. It would break my heart to have to part with any of them, but I might have to do it to pay the nursing home one of these days. My kids are not musicians, so maybe they'll end up selling them.

Any advice for our younger readers?

A great way to get rich is to collect things that are scarce, whether that's instruments or rare coins or houses on the beach. If they're not making any more of it, it should go up a lot in value over time. And only collect things that you know a lot about. If I had been collecting rare coins, instead of guitars, I probably would have gotten cheated.

Any other advice?

Take care of your body when you're young. That's something I could have done better. Get lots of sleep and exercise, and eat your veggies. And don't forget to spend some time doing those things you really love. I can't imagine my life without music. You only get one shot at this life, so make it a good one.

Thanks for taking the time to talk with me today.

16

THE BITCOIN MILLIONAIRE

I usually begin these interviews by asking about your early life. In your case, I'd like to begin with a description of your current existence, since it is so fascinating.

These days, I spend about 40% of my time in Airbnb residences around the world, and 60% on cruises. All of my worldly possessions fit inside my backpack: a toothbrush, an iPhone, a MacBook Pro, and some clothes. My current net worth is north of $5 million. I guess you could call it the digital monk lifestyle.

Do you have a favorite country that you like to visit?

Definitely Thailand. I love the people, the vibe, and the food. Thailand has one of the best food cultures in the world. The food is aromatic, and full of ingredients that are medicinally beneficial. Thailand also has some of the world's best Vipassana meditation retreats.

What is Vipassana?

Vipassana is a Theravada Buddhist form of meditation. The word Vipassana can be translated as "insight." Vipassana meditation allows you to see reality as it really is. These days our minds are clouded by social media and other online distractions. Many of us are already living the life of cyborgs, permanently tethered to our phones. We know how to tap into the collective wisdom of the internet, but we don't know how to express our fullest human potential. That can only be achieved by quieting our minds and viewing reality as it is.

What does a Vipassana retreat involve?

It's quite painful the first time. You have to meditate for ten hours every day for ten days, while on a strict vegetarian diet. No electronics, no reading, no writing, and no speaking to anyone at the retreat. But you emerge on the other side with your mind sparkling clean and shimmering with clarity. There's nothing like it.

How did you become a millionaire?

I was born and grew up in New Jersey. I attended a small college in California, was studying economics, but then ran out of money before I could get my degree. So I moved back to New Jersey, and back into my childhood room in my parents' house. It was extremely humiliating. My parents are wonderful people, but that was not exactly the trajectory that I had been hoping for.

I spent the next few years bouncing around from job to job. I had a lot of intellectual interests, including economics and software, but could never find a way to translate them into a higher-paying job. I was usually just a zombie at work, but then came alive when I came home from work. I used to spend whole weekends reading financial and economic blogs.

Pretty soon my 5-year high school reunion was on its way. Here I was, with a lot of credit card debt, with a crappy job, and still living with my parents. I was a proud intellectual explorer by night, but still a loser by day.

So I decided to skip the official high school reunion and instead go out drinking with old friends afterwards. My self-esteem had definitely reached its nadir at this point. As the night went on, I got pretty drunk.

Then my friends began to pass around the weed. Having no self-control, I quickly succumbed. Now I was drunk, stoned, and thoroughly numbed. I stumbled home and went straight for my computer.

As I sat there at the computer, something really strange happened. My point of view shifted, and all of a sudden I could see myself seated at my desk, staring at the screen. It was some sort of astral projection or drug-induced illusion.

I was somehow browsing Reddit alongside my inebriated corporeal self, but I could tell that I was observing things at a much deeper level. I was observing things at a more spiritual level, which seemed to allow me to ignore the online distractions and instead browse with an almost divine purpose. I was navigating through Reddit and knew exactly where I was going, even though at the same time I had no idea where I was going. Some things can only be expressed through the language of paradox.

Then I began to read about Bitcoin for the first time. I was drunk and stoned, but it made perfect sense. It may have been my libertarian background that had already prepared my mind to understand Bitcoin.

Here was a new currency that was easy to transact in, that was beyond the control of governments, and that had a permanently fixed supply. It seemed strange that my drug-induced mystical experience would culminate on a discussion website with a chance encounter with a new digital currency. But that's what happened. I knew immediately that I needed to buy some Bitcoin right away. And I knew that it would make me rich.

What year was this?

This was early 2011. I took all of the money that I had at the time ($900) and bought 900 bitcoins at around $1 each. I remember that it took me a couple of days just to figure out how to buy them. There were no exchanges like Coinbase back then.

Soon after my purchase, Bitcoin soared from $1 to above $30, only to crash back down to about $2 a few months later. I tried not to watch it, since I didn't trust myself. I knew that this was something that I had to hold on to for the long term.

How did you know this?

I knew it at both an intellectual level, and at a spiritual level.

At an intellectual level, I realized from my reading that these bitcoins were essentially a perpetual option on the crypto future. They were either going to zero (in which case, I would lose the entire $900), or they were going much much higher. For that reason, it didn't make sense to try to jump in and out of the trade.

At a spiritual level, I simply knew that I had to hold. The impression from my vision that night was and still is very vivid to me. I certainly don't recommend getting drunk or smoking pot. Knowing what I know now, I think you can accomplish the same thing much more safely with meditation.

At today's prices ($6,200), those 900 Bitcoin are now worth about $5.6 million. I've sold some of them to pay for expenses in the meantime, so my current stake is worth about $5 million.

What are you currently invested in?

I still have 99% of my net worth in Bitcoin. For better or worse, I'm sticking with this one, which has been really good to me. I only sell off a bit here or there to pay my expenses, which these days are minimal. Whenever possible, I try to always transact in Bitcoin directly. I can't wait until Airbnb and every cruise line start accepting Bitcoin.

Why do you spend so much time on cruises?

A cruise is to travel what meditation is to daily life. I love being at sea, surrounded by only the clouds above and the blue ocean below.

Everything is taken care of. You can eat anytime you want. There are huge blocks of time for writing, or reading quietly without distractions. There are always interesting people to meet, or you can spend the day alone.

I don't drink alcohol any more or party, so my experience of cruise ships may be different from most. My favorite cruises are the transoceanic cruises, where you get to spend most of your time at sea. Stopping at exotic foreign ports can be fun, but real peace can only be found far from land.

What a lot of people don't realize is that it is often cheaper to live on a cruise ship than it is to live on land. I sometimes use

CruiseSheet.com to find the best deals. I just got back from a cruise that cost me only $35 per day, and that included a room, all meals, entertainment, port fees, and taxes. I enjoy living simply and getting a great deal like that. And sometimes I also enjoy splurging and staying in the owner's suite or penthouse-- especially if I am traveling with my girlfriend and she wants to have a grand piano in the room.

Have you ever thought of settling down somewhere and putting down roots?

Yes, I have. The problem is that houses are a pretty illiquid asset. Furthermore, they are expensive to maintain, and when you own one, you are tempted to fill it with useless things that you don't really need. Too often our possessions end up owning us.

I like the freedom of a minimalist lifestyle. I find that it frees my mind. I don't have to remember to pay the gardener or have him blow out the sprinklers before the freeze sets in. I don't have to be irritated every time I see the paint on my house starting to peel. That frees up a lot of mental RAM for other things.

The great advantage of travel is that it provides a built-in change of external stimuli. When you stay in the same place, your mind keeps its same patterns. When you travel, your mind is forced into new patterns.

Have you ever noticed how your mind feels when you get

back to your house after a vacation? You see everything in a fresh light and with a new perspective. You feel recharged and re-energized. That's how I feel all of the time. Travel keeps my brain growing and curious.

Thanks for taking the time to talk with me today.

17

THE CANDLE MAKER

Tell us a little bit about your early life.

I grew up in small town in eastern Washington. My father was a farmer, and my mother was your traditional farmer's wife. My father primarily grew wheat, but we also had a big family vegetable garden, as well as some fruit trees.

I remember my mother spending much of the summer and fall drying herbs, canning vegetables, and making fruit jams and jellies. As with any other crop, there were booms and busts in wheat, but we were able to ride them out by keeping our debt low and by growing much of our own food.

My mother was also a master candle maker, a craft that she learned from her mother who was born in Norway. My mother used to sell her candles at county fairs, which provided another source of income for our family.

I helped my mother make candles every year, but never thought much about it.

After high school, I went to a local college, got married, and had children. Years passed.

Then late one night when I was watching TV, I saw a show on candle making. A flood of memories came back from my childhood, and I really wanted to make some homemade candles again.

I bought a large double boiler, some candle wax and wicks, and started making candles again while my kids were at school. I began to remember a lot of the Old World tricks that my mother had taught me. And I began to experiment with using different ingredients.

Most candles that you buy at the store are made with paraffin wax, which is a petroleum product. When you burn paraffin, you get many of the same toxic air byproducts that you would expect from a petroleum product.

I started making my candles with soy wax or beeswax, which are much more clean-burning than paraffin candles. And both soy wax and beeswax are renewable resources, unlike paraffin.

Also, I've never liked the artificial smells that many candles come in. I just don't think it's natural for a candle to smell like chocolate cake or blueberry muffins. There's no natural way to get fragrances like that, so you really are breathing in a lot of chemicals when you burn one of them.

I began to make my candles using essential oils, and other natural fragrances.

My friends and family loved these candles. I began to hand them out as birthday gifts, or I'd bring them instead of a bottle of wine when we went to a dinner party.

People kept telling me that I should open up a store to sell my candles. I didn't like the idea of leasing space and being outside of the home. Part of the joy was being able to cook these things up in my kitchen while I watched TV.

Finally, a friend told me about Etsy. So I decided to give it a try. I put up a couple of candles, and was amazed when they sold immediately. Then I began to receive messages asking when I would have more candles available.

What year was this?

Early 2014. Our business has been growing ever since. As the business grew, I finally gave in and leased a small warehouse near our house, as well as hired a few employees. Now that my kids are older, I can devote more time to the business.

Where do you get most of your traffic?

At this point, it's definitely from Facebook and Instagram.

Do you still sell on Etsy?

Yes. We also have our own website hosted on Shopify. They make it so easy. You just pick a theme, upload some pictures, and descriptions, and you're ready to go. Shopify takes care of all of the payment processing, inventory management, etc.

How much money have you made since 2014?

We've taken home more than a million dollars. I never would have guessed it was possible just from selling candles.

Do you have any advice for a stay-at-home mom who would like to start a business?

My best advice is just to get started. Make something and then immediately try to sell it to someone, whether it's online or at a farmers market. Don't waste time registering a business and designing a logo until you have a product that you are sure will sell.

More people fail by never getting started than fail by making a business mistake. Once you actually get started, you'll get a much better feel for what people want to buy.

Also don't be afraid to be yourself, especially online. There's no need to try to imitate famous brands, since many people prefer homemade brands over sterile commercial brands.

Thanks for taking the time to talk with me today.

18

THE MILLIONAIRE ARTIST

Tell us a little bit about your early life.

I was born and grew up in the Midwest, where I still live. I was one of those kids who was always drawing. When I was a toddler, I used to steal pens or crayons and draw all over the walls of our house. My parents were very patient with their little budding artist. I've always known that God put me on this earth to draw things. When I was a bit older, I learned how to confine my drawings to a piece of paper. Still later, I was introduced to Adobe Photoshop, and was completely blown away by what it could do.

Did you attend college?

I went to a well-known art school in the Midwest, and focused on graphic design. After graduating, I got a job at a local graphic design agency. We were focused on website design, as well as some book design.

Was the book design for traditional publishers?

Yes, at the beginning. Then I began to see the shift towards self-publishing. I am an avid reader, and had bought one of the first Kindles, so I was familiar with what Amazon was doing with self-publishing from the beginning.

After my first few years at the agency, I began to do more and more Kindle book covers for self-published authors. I wasn't making that much money at the agency at the time, but I was seeing how much these book covers were selling for.

About six months later, I got married. At the time, my husband had a job that paid well, which gave me some flexibility to think about my future. I had really begun to love designing ebook covers. One day while I was cooking dinner, I made the decision: I was going to strike out on my own and devote myself to designing eBook covers.

How did you get your first clients?

My first clients came from Fiverr. They were all authors who were self-publishing their books on Amazon. It was very time-consuming going back and forth with the client. They would first fill out a questionnaire to give me an idea what kind of book cover they were looking for. Then I would present a couple of ideas. Sometimes they would like one of them, but more often than not I had to come up with multiple designs, and then multiple revisions, before they were satisfied. It was a lot of work for just $5-10.

What was the next step?

In my free time, I was always spending a lot of time on Amazon and Pinterest checking out new book cover ideas. I would look at the best-selling books in each category and see what the covers had in common. When I was driving or cooking or lying in bed, my mind would keep coming up with new ideas for book covers, based on what I was learning.

One day when I was out for a jog, I had a flash of inspiration. Why not just post all of my ideas online? I could create a simple website and put all of my new ebook covers on it. If someone came across them and wanted to buy one, that would be great, but originally it was just a way for me to catalogue the covers that I was creating. I also began posting my designs on Pinterest and Facebook, and then linking back to my website.

How did you know how to setup a website?

It was pretty simple actually. I bought the domain and hosted it on HostGator. They made it really easy to use Wordpress, which I'm still using today. Whenever I had a question about how to do something I just googled it.

When did you get your first sale?

A few months after setting up the website, I got an email from someone who actually wanted to buy one of the book covers that he had seen on the website. I asked him how much he was willing to pay, and he said $50. So he sent me the money through PayPal, and I emailed him the design files.

Shortly after this, I added a simple PayPal button to my website. All you had to do was pay $50, and then send me a separate email telling me which book cover you wanted. I would then quickly personalize it by adding the title and author's name to the cover.

Soon my website began to show up in people's Google searches. A few blogs and podcasts in the self-publishing space began to link to my site too. My business has only grown from there.

How much money are you making these days?

I currently charge anywhere from $50 to $100 for a book cover. I usually sell about 10 covers every day, so I'm making about $500 to $1,000 daily. It's pure profit, except for the 3% that I pay PayPal on every transaction.

Do you reuse book covers?

Never. I have so many ideas that it's not necessary. I can sit down and design 20 new book covers on a good day, while watching a movie on Netflix.

Are you a millionaire yet?

Yes, it's still hard for me to believe it, but I am. I've made more than a million dollars in the last 6 years after taxes.

Where do you invest your money?

I have all of my money invested in VTSAX, which is the Vanguard Total Stock Market Index Fund. The expense ratio is just 0.04 percent, and it gives me exposure to all U.S. stocks. After reading your Warren Buffett book, I plan on buying some Buffett stocks going forward as well.

Any final words of wisdom for the reader?

Yes, try to always be doing work in an industry that is growing. If you are working in a shrinking industry, you have a headwind that you are always fighting. Much better to have the tailwind of growth. The eBook industry is still growing quite rapidly, and I think it has many years of growth ahead of it.

We are very lucky to live at this time in history. With some hard work and a little luck, even a humble artist can become a millionaire.

Thanks for taking the time to talk with me today.

19

BONUS CHAPTER: AIRBNB ARBITRAGE

Can you tell us a little bit about your Airbnb strategy?

Yes, it's definitely a strategy that's been working well in my local market. I stumbled on this idea when my roommate moved out and I had a spare room to sublease out. Instead of getting another long-term renter, I decided to put it on Airbnb instead.

For your readers who haven't yet heard of Airbnb, it is a short-term rental or vacation rental website. If you own a house, you can rent out the whole house as a vacation rental. You can also rent out a spare room in your house on a nightly basis.

If it helps, you can think of it as basically like running your own mini-hotel. The great thing is that Airbnb takes care of all of the payments, booking, cancelling, etc. You post your listing on their website, complete with pictures and a description, and Airbnb takes care of the rest-- including finding you overnight guests and screening them to make sure that they are not criminals. Airbnb only charges hosts a 3% fee, so the great news is that you get to keep 97% of what you charge.

So what happened?

In my area, a private bedroom and attached bath goes for about $1,000/month. That is what my previous roommate had been paying. Now when I started looking on Airbnb, I noticed that similar listings were going for about $60 per night. That's when my eureka moment hit. If I could rent out that room on a nightly basis about 85% of the time, I would be collecting $60/night times 30 days in a month times 85% or $1,530 per month. Subtract the 3% Airbnb fee, and I would be left with $1,484 per month.

Now I only needed to collect $1,000 from that room to pay my landlord. So I could pocket the extra $484/month for very little work. At the time, I needed to pay $1,000 for my private bedroom and bath in the house, so my effective rent was now only $516 per month.

So you're basically doing an arbitrage between the long-term rental rate and the short-term rental rate?

Exactly. The good news is that on Airbnb, the guest pays for the cleaning fee as well, so that $484 was pure profit for me. That's when the lightbulb went on for me. Why not find another 2 bedroom/2 bath house to rent in my neighborhood, get permission from the landlord to put it on Airbnb, and then list those 2 private bedrooms on Airbnb? If I could make the same profit per room, that would net me another $968 per month.

Were you able to do that?

At first, no. Then I discovered better ways of talking to prospective landlords. Offer to pay an extra hundred dollars per month above what he is asking. Tell him that you will only be renting to non-smokers and people without pets. Tell him that the house will be professionally cleaned every 1-2 days. Also, offer to take out an additional insurance policy on the house. This will not cost you much, and the landlord will be very happy to have an extra layer of insurance on his house.

Did that work?

Yes, it worked like a charm. I was able take out long-term leases on 5 additional houses. Each house is now netting me approximately $870 per month, so that's an extra $4,350 per month that I am now making. I've installed electronic smart locks on all of the houses (with the landlord's permission, of course), so it's very easy to change the code after each guest leaves. And that way I don't have to worry about physical keys, or meeting up with each guest individually. All 5 houses are professionally cleaned after a guest leaves, and the guest themselves pay for this cleaning fee on Airbnb. I am now making enough money that I have been able to quit my day job. It's a dream come true.

Would you be willing to tell us where you live?

No. I really wish that I could, but I'm scared that it will create too much competition for me. I've browsed online, and it looks like this strategy will work in many different cities all over the U.S. If you can stick to places that are clearly tourist destinations, I think that your profits will be even higher.

Do you have plans to scale this business?

Yes, if this works for 5 houses, why not do it with 50 houses? At that point, I would be making $43,500 **per month**, even with just an 85% occupancy rate. The only problem is all of the texts and phone calls that I get from my guests. For example, they ask me how to use the cable TV, where the hairdryer is, where the fusebox is, etc.

I'm currently investigating ways to outsource this. There are online services that will take care of all of this for you, for a reasonable fee. If I can spread this fee over multiple houses, I think it will be definitely worth it. That way my guests will have access to a 24/7 help desk. Almost like the front desk of a hotel, except that it will be servicing all of my houses. I am excited to see where I can take this business. I think the sky's the limit.

Congratulations. It's a very clever idea, and I hope it continues to pay you in spades. Thanks for agreeing to share your strategy with my readers.

20

FROM SMALL BEGINNINGS TO GREAT WEALTH

I hope that you've enjoyed these interviews with self-made millionaires.

If you have, be sure to check out my other books here:

www.trader-books.com

I have certainly enjoyed doing these interviews, and I have learned a lot in the process.

Whenever I read a new book like this, I try to figure out some concrete steps that I can immediately take to put the lessons that I've learned into action.

Now it's time for you to take action too.

Don't just put this book down and do nothing.

Start to take steps every day that will bring you closer to becoming a millionaire.

Start to spend a little bit less money, and save a bit more.

Maybe open up a brokerage account, and start buying some stocks.

Maybe start your own YouTube channel, or register a domain and start a blog.

If you keep doing what you have always been doing, you'll probably be in the same place 5 years from now.

Don't let that happen.

By the way, thanks for purchasing this book and reading it all the way to the end.

If you enjoyed this book and found it useful, I'd be very grateful if you'd post an honest review on Amazon.

All that you need to do is to **click here** (or go to www.trader-books.com) and then click on the correct book cover.

Then click the blue link next to the yellow stars that says "customer reviews."

You'll then see a gray button that says "Write a customer review"—click that and you're good to go.

Also, if you would like to learn more ways to make money, check out my other books on the next page.

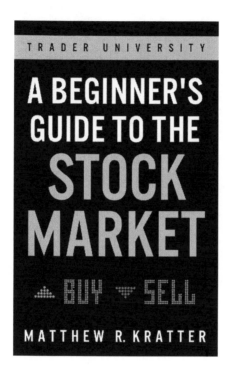

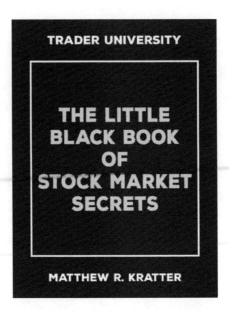

Click here to buy this book on Amazon

Or simply go to www.trader-books.com

YOUR FREE GIFT

Thanks for buying my book!

As a way of showing my appreciation, I would like to share with you a FREE Bonus Chapter:

"The 30 Habits of Self-Made Millionaires"

This bonus chapter is a great summary of everything that I've learned while interviewing self-made millionaires, as well as habits from my own life that have helped to make me successful.

To get your free copy, go here now:

https://www.trader.university/habits

ABOUT THE AUTHOR

Hi there!

My name is Matthew Kratter.

I am the founder of Trader University (www.trader.university), where I offer online courses about how to make money in stocks, options, futures, and crypto.

I have more than 20 years of trading experience, including working at multiple hedge funds.

I know how professional traders and investors think and approach the markets.

And I am committed to sharing their trading strategies with you in my books and courses.

Be sure to check out my YouTube channel here:

https://www.youtube.com/trader-university

When I am not trading or writing new books, I enjoy skiing and hiking in the mountains with my wife, kids, and dogs.

DISCLAIMER

While the author has used his best efforts in preparing this book, he makes no representations or warranties with respect to the accuracy or completeness of the contents of this book and specifically disclaims any implied warranties or merchantability or fitness for a particular purpose. The advice and strategies contained herein may not be suitable for your situation.

You should consult with a legal, financial, tax, health or other professional where appropriate. Neither the publisher nor the author shall be liable for any loss of profit or any other commercial damages, including but not limited to special, incidental, consequential, or other damages.

This book is for educational purposes only. The views expressed are those of the author alone, and should not be taken as expert instruction or commands. The reader is responsible for his or her own actions.

Adherence to all applicable laws and regulations, including international, federal, state, and local laws, is the sole responsibility of the purchaser or reader.

Neither the author nor the publisher assumes any responsibility or liability whatsoever on the behalf of the purchaser or reader of these materials.

Any perceived slight of any individual or organization is purely unintentional.

Past performance is not necessarily indicative of future performance.

Forex, futures, stock, and options trading is not appropriate for everyone.

There is a substantial risk of loss associated with trading these markets. Losses can and will occur.

No system or methodology has ever been developed that can guarantee profits or ensure freedom from losses. Nor will it likely ever be.

No representation or implication is being made that using the methodologies or systems or the information contained within this book will generate profits or ensure freedom from losses.

The information contained in this book is for educational purposes only and should NOT be taken as investment advice. Examples presented here are not solicitations to buy or sell. The author, publisher, and all affiliates assume no responsibility for your trading results.

There is a high risk in trading.

HYPOTHETICAL OR SIMULATED PERFORMANCE RESULTS HAVE CERTAIN LIMITATIONS.

UNLIKE AN ACTUAL PERFORMANCE RECORD, SIMU-LATED RESULTS DO NOT REPRESENT ACTUAL TRAD-ING. ALSO, SINCE THE TRADES HAVE NOT BEEN EXECUTED, THE RESULTS MAY HAVE UNDER-OR-OVER COMPENSATED FOR THE IMPACT, IF ANY, OF CERTAIN MARKET FACTORS, SUCH AS THE LACK OF LIQUIDITY.

SIMULATED TRADING PROGRAMS IN GENERAL ARE ALSO SUBJECT TO THE FACT THAT THEY ARE DESIGNED WITH THE BENEFIT OF HINDSIGHT. NO REPRESENTATION IS BEING MADE THAT ANY ACCOUNT WILL OR IS LIKELY TO ACHIEVE PROFIT OR LOSSES SIMILAR TO THOSE SHOWN.

Made in the USA
Middletown, DE
09 May 2020